D0081307

MASS ADVERTISING AS SOCIAL FORECAST

A method for futures research

WITHDRAWN FROM UNIVERSITY OF PENNSYLVANIA LIBRARIES

JIB FOWLES

MASS ADVERTISING AS SOCIAL FORECAST

A method for futures research

GREENWOOD PRESS
Westport, Connecticut • London, England

HN
59
F66

Library of Congress Cataloging in Publication Data

Fowles, Jib.
  Mass advertising as social forecast.

  Bibliography: p.
  Includes index.
  1. Social prediction. 2. United States—Social conditions 1960-   3. Ad-
vertising—United States. I. Title.
HN59.F66   659.1'9'309173   75-35344
ISBN 0-8371-8595-5

Copyright © 1976 by Robert B. Fowles

All rights reserved. No portion of this book may be reproduced, by any
process or technique, without the express written consent of the publisher.

Library of Congress Catalog Card Number: 75-35344
ISBN: 0-8371-8595-5

First published in 1976

Greenwood Press, a division of Williamhouse-Regency Inc.
51 Riverside Avenue, Westport, Connecticut 06880

Printed in the United States of America

UNIVERSITY
OF
PENNSYLVANIA
LIBRARIES

For my parents

C98164

"The social student of the future will pore over the inclusive dramas embodied in our advertisements. . . ."

Marshall McLuhan, **Culture Is Our Business**

Contents

Tables

MASS ADVERTISING AS SOCIAL FORECAST

A method for futures research

CHAPTER 1

The study of the future: dimensions and deficiencies

THE NEED FOR KNOWLEDGE OF THE FUTURE

Man is time's creature. Other animals make do with short memories and little foresight, but human lives are lavishly temporal. "All distinctively human attributes derive from awareness of what has gone before and expectation of what is to come."[1] This special intimacy with time, no matter how incomplete, has helped to elevate the lot of mankind above the rest of the species.

Awareness of what has gone before, stored in images and symbols, contributes both stability and versatility to the human venture. How things have been done is one part of the inheritance, but how things could be done if need be is another. The accumulation of experience permits not only social order but also adaptive responses. As a result cultures have come to be resilient and extensive, and societies bulk ever larger in population and elaborateness.

And in the other direction, the complexity of human life is also sustained through expectation of what is to come. "The very possibility of social organization," commented Otis Dudley Duncan, "rests on our ability to anticipate correctly, in a large proportion of instances, the behavior of others. Society, from this point of view, is an intricate reticulation of expectations and commitments concerning future actions and reactions."[2] Thus much of the future is treated as if it were certain, which, for all practical purposes, it is. Every person is bound into recognized and unrecognized obligations that order the time ahead.

But more is tantalizingly, fearfully, not certain. Over the centuries, in the attempt to know the fate of men and nations, great effort has been spent at prevision. The instrumentalities were those at hand: magic and occultism for primitive beings, religion in theological periods, and science in behalf of modern man. As for the last, "the undertaking of conscious and systematic forecasting is simply an attempt to effect improvement in a natural activity of the mind," said Bertrand de Jouvenel in his highly regarded examination of the logical and philosophical underpinnings of prediction, *The Art of Conjecture.*[3]

Science is being brought to bear at a time when the demand for knowledge of the future has risen to a new pitch. This concern is signaled by the popularity of such books as Herman Kahn and Anthony J. Wiener's *The Year 2000* and Alvin Toffler's *Future Shock,* as well as by the growth of the futurists' organization, the World Future Society, from 200 members in 1967 to 12,000 in 1973.[4] The widespread desire to know more about what the future will bring stems from increasing change in the patterns of modern life, de Jouvenel explained.

> Our modern civilization has repudiated the sacredness of institutions and commitments, and therewith the means of achieving a known future. As we have loosened our guaranteed holds on the future, so have we facilitated change and made the future unknown. Clearly, we have far fewer certainties about the future of our civilization than the Chinese once had about the future of theirs. The great problem of our age is that we want things to change more rapidly, and at the same time we want to have a better knowledge of things to come.[5]

More traditional peoples, in thrall to their conventions and prescriptions, have presumably less need for information about the future than do the participants in an unsettled contemporary life.

Of course, there is more than apprehension behind the growing popular interest in what is to come. The exploration of the future affords an opportunity to unlimber imaginations. People who enjoy speculation enjoy matching their intuitions with the views of those who professionally study the future.

However, currently the most insistent demands for knowledge of the future come not from the general public but from large-scale organizations, which are part and parcel of the changing social landscape. Kenneth Boulding wrote, "Not only are there many more organizations, and many more kinds of organizations, than a century previous, but the organizations themselves are larger, better organized, more closely knit, more efficient in the arts of attracting members and funds in pursuing their multitudinous ends."[6] The benchmark of changing times, these organizations—military, governmental, manufacturing, marketing, service, and so on—must also anticipate change if they are to ensure their own well-being. "What has virtually forced the new futurism into existence," it has been observed, "is the extraordinary bigness, the piles of money at stake, and the complexity of intersecting interests involved in almost any significant corporation or government operation or project."[7] For these gigantic operations to meet varying requirements for what they offer and what they as a consequence need, and for them to see to it that their internal components run smoothly and productively, they must have the clearest possible foreknowledge; only then can adept planning go on. As the dimensions of public and private organizations have swelled since World War II, therefore, a larger proportion of their resources have been allocated to anticipation and plans.[8] The result is improved forecasting, improved planning, and more vigorous organizations with still greater appetites for knowledge of the future.

In brief, modern life is predicated on the viability of enormous organizations whose concerns stretch out not only in space but in time. The operations of these organizations are the sum of countless decisions, decisions improved through awareness of what is impending. It is as an aid to decision-making that the study of the future finds its soberest function.[9]

THE RISE OF FUTURES RESEARCH

Public and corporate care for the future is calling into being a prognostic discipline which de Jouvenel pronounced "a field of activity that is to be systematic, disciplined, justifiable, and discussable."[10] The field is now starting to come into its own, rising from modest beginnings in the 1940s.

To some extent this new endeavor was the off-spring of a long if weakened strain of sociology: "sociology grew out of a concern with prediction (Comte's *savoir pour prevoir*) and has always had the securing of predictive knowledge as one of its express aims."[11] Until fifty years ago such social thinkers as Saint-Simon, Comte, Spencer, de Tocqueville, Marx, Weber, and Durkheim were unafraid of the sweeping prophetic concepts which twentieth century sociologists have largely shunned.[12] Interest in prediction in the large was subsequently blanketed by devotion to explanation in the small. It was widely felt that the social sciences should achieve a finer understanding of how society works before venturing how it will work. Thus since 1920, as attention turned from the diachronic to the synchronic, narrower, more approachable, topics typified sociology.[13]

This was the state of affairs when, near the end of World War II, an article by Ossip Flechtheim appeared which proposed a "scientific prognosis" of man's future.[14] This piece has prompted some to think of Flechtheim as "the founding father of modern futurism."[15] Several years later Flechtheim recalled,

> In 1945, I suggested the new term "futurology" in the United States in order to stress the importance of a scholarly interest in the future of man and his culture. What I then called the new futurological approach was the attempt to discuss the evolution of man and his society in the hitherto forbidden future tense. I held that, by marshalling the ever growing resources of science and scholarship, we could do more than employ retrospective analysis and hypothetical predictions; we could

try to establish the degree of credibility and probability of forecasts.[16]

It has proved to be a challenge increasingly heard.

But in the last analysis neither sociology's traditions nor Flechtheim's exhortations provided much of substance for the new science of the future. The means most frequently identified with futures research came from more prosaic sources—from operations research and systems analysis which had their inception in the military exigencies of World War II, and which evolved as the Cold War did.[17] It is their contribution which allows the study of the future—as some thing more than an intriguing concept—to be dated from the 1940s. Without the attitudes, procedures, and personnel taken over from these fields, the science of the future would have languished.

It did not, although through the 1950s the field remained ill-defined, and those in government, industry, and the academic world who were working on the problems of forecasing had little contact with one another.[18] In the sixties, though, a critical mass was reached and the study of the future bloomed. Abruptly it assumed all the legitimating trappings: conferences were organized one after the other, and institutes were founded in rapid succession. In Austria Robert Jungk established the Institute für Zukunftsfragen; in Paris de Jouvenel started up the Futuribles research association; in the United Kingdom the Social Research Council spawned the Committee on the Next Thirty Years; and the American Academy of Arts and Science created the Commission on the Year 2000 under the leadership of Daniel Bell.[19] This growth has continued rapidly until the present day, reaching the point where Theodore Gordon of the Institute for the Future could expansively claim, "The published literature in the field is now so extensive that no single person could follow it all."[20]

Today there are any number of periodicals which print articles to do with the study of the future, and at least six reputable English-language journals are devoted to the subject: *The Futurist*, from the World Future Society; *Futures*, largely concerned with methodological questions, from England; *Technological Forecasting and Social Change* (previously just *Technological Forecasting*); *Long-Range Planning*; *Fields Within Fields*; and *Working Papers for a New Society*. Over 350 courses on the future are now given in American colleges and universities.[21] The number of people who actually earn their living as futurists has been estimated at 1,000 by John McHale in his recent canvass of the field.[22] It has been calculated that corporations now allocate upwards of $50 billion a year to forecasting efforts.[23] Probing the future, then, has quickly become a substantial enterprise.

And, in the eyes of some, a successful one. "The fact is that forecasting, with all its problems, is becoming increasingly more scientific and accurate as the problems of scouting the future have been identified, and forecasting tools have multiplied and become refined," one observer stated.[24] Since it is better for a decision-maker to have a forecast in hand than not to have one, futurists are coming to have considerable influence upon policy-making.[25]

But for all its achievements, it is a comment on the immaturity of the field that as yet there exists no commonly accepted name for it. "Futurology," the term originally proposed by Flechtheim, was rejected by de Jouvenel because it suggested an unobtainable scientific rigor.[26] Circumspectly, de Jouvenel spoke of an "art of conjecture" which dealt with "futuribles," or the array of possible outcomes.[27] Nevertheless, Herman Kahn appears to have accepted "futurology,"[28] and he is not alone. "Futurism" is also in vogue, used by Alvin Toffler[29] and others. Fred Polak proposed "prognostics" in a book by the same name,[30] and it is reported this label has caught on in Communist countires.[31] The president of the World Future Society settled on "futuristics" after some reflection,[32] lending support to that claimant. But the leading contender at the moment seems to be "futures research," used more and more at conferences and in publications. Perhaps it is found attractive because it suggests on the one hand an open-mindedness to a range of possible developments, and on the other, aspirations to objectivity. In any case, to lift a sentence from John McHale, "Futures research is the preferred term used in the present study."[33]

THE CHARACTERISTICS OF FORECASTS

"It is not a science of the future which is rising," someone noted shrewdly, "but a science of the laws and methods of forecasting."[34] No doubt he made the distinction because he recognized a unique and fundamentally troublesome attribute of futures research: it is the only science whose subject matter by definition does not exist. There is nowhere one can turn to if one wishes to scrutinize the future. Such an irredeemable condition, it can be argued, means that scientific statements about the future are improbable.

> Scientific method is to do with the generation of hypotheses, the collection of relevant data and the comparison of the hypotheses with data. It still remains to be seen how far these traditional procedures of science may be applied to future studies. At the moment, all we can say is that a very great deal of uncertainty surrounds the application of the first two and that that of the third—the comparison of hypotheses with the 'reality' represented by *future* data—is, by definition, impossible.[35]

Nevertheless, François Hetman, the lexicographer of the field, proclaimed, "Future research is a scientific quest."[36] Forecasts, the stuff of futures research, are to be as scientific as conditions permit.

It is the concept of probability which allows forecasters to sensibly confront the conundrum of the nonexistence of their subject.[37] Forecasts are generically probabilistic in recognition of the fact that the future affords no certainties. With degrees of likelihood stated, a decided improvement is achieved over the situation of having either a categorical statement or no categorical statement. If the probabilities are not explicit, they are implicit, which comes to mean that forecasts are characterized by their tentativeness, as are all statements with scientific pretensions. It is plausibilities that forecasts deal in.

Degrees of likelihood often get associated with a number of possible developments. These possibilities, or alternative futures, are what de Jouvenel christened "futuribles." Some futuribles are bound to be more likely than others, but all are to be given due attention. (Conceptions of various futures are treated reverently in futures research; one of the very few things that all futurists can agree upon is that the stock of futuribles should always be open to newcomers, and that none should be screened out prematurely. There is good reason involved in this tenet, certainly, but there is more. One cannot help being reminded of something Henri Bergson said: "The idea of the future, pregnant with an infinity of possibilities, is thus more fruitful than the future itself, and this is why we find more charm in hope than in possession, in dreams than in reality."[38])

It is not enough that a forecast be tentative and made with an awareness of the alternatives. If it is to have any standing, it must also be rationalized through the futurist's fullest explanation of the dynamics of the system under study and of his methods for investigating it. A forecast "should be accompanied by the intellectual scaffolding which supports it; this 'construct' must be transparent and articulated, and subjected to criticism."[39] Forecasts come with reasons.

Another attribute of forecasts is that, to be of maximum utility, they are often laid out along a gradient of time. The forecast period is frequently less than three years.

Forecasts, in summary, are readily contrasted with other orders of statements about the future. They are dispassionate in intention while others are infused with values and hopes; they are probabilistic and provisional, while others are absolute; they are couched in terms of method and rationale, while others arise from inspiration and are simply asserted. Forecasts are generally thought to be more exacting than predictions (although the word "prediction" may creep in here from time to time for stylistic relief).[40] And, even though some feel otherwise,[41] forecasts do not include plans, or so-called normative forecasts,[42] which pertain to definite present designs more than to plausible future developments, and which are drawn up after forecasts are made.

THE TWO SECTORS OF THE FUTURE

Futurists argue that, like it or not, we are now in effect creating the future with our decisions, discoveries, actions, and inactions. Since we are creating the future, they contend, we are in a position to determine at least part of it. By looking at what possible alternative futures can or should be, the futurists feel that they can give to the rest of us the perception to make better decisions about the future we want rather than the one that engulfs us because of our own haphazard actions.

Specifically, the futurist believes that he can have an impact where expenditures of time, money, energy, and thought can conspire to cause some events and prevent others. They agree that some aspects of all futures are beyond our control.[43]

Hardly visible in this passage is a gesture toward a crucial but insufficiently discussed difficulty to do with the nature of the future and the nature of forecasting. What is commonly thought of as the future is in actuality only a portion of the whole. This portion is the area where human will may be exercised; in this selection, as in the field, it receives the greater part of the attention. The second portion is what the writer, as an afterthought, referred to as "beyond our control"; it is also beyond the interests of most futurists, although it is momentous.

Taking the whole to be the future of a socio-cultural system, one of its two parts consists of all the matters which are susceptible to human intervention. Examples are external relations, internal governance, the management of economies, business, environmental affairs, developments in theoretical and applied knowledge, the education of new members. This is the realm where control can be exercised—the volitional sector. It is manifest reality; it is what the news covers. Most futurists, in service to the decision-makers of government and industry, probe here.

The volitional sector is embedded in the nonvolitional sector, which is conceived as being by far the larger of the two and by far the less well known. In this second area belong the grand dynamics which so far are impervious to determination of men. To Albert and Donna Wilson these are "the recognizable patterns of social change. They are the processes such as the natural growth of economies, populations, and institutions that provide the continuity of society."[44] These forces suffuse the volitional sector and alter its tenor, so that, for instance, the late 1920s and the late 1960s have a different cast to them than surrounding periods.

Seeing the future as composed of these two sectors goes some little ways toward resolving a continuing squabble in futures research. Robert Theobald set futurists into two camps—the objectivists, who argue "that the future is determined by the past," and the subjectivists, who feel "that the world is more or less totally malleable."[45]

Given the division of the future into the volitional and nonvolitional sectors, they are both correct. The subjectivists would have to agree that they could do little to alter the course of massive cultural change, or modifications in symbol systems, or the patterns of human desires. And the objectivists must admit that volition can produce communes, highways, marketing plans, the SST, and the termination of the SST.

Recognition of the two sectors logically leads to a call for two branches of futures research. Yujiro Hayashi proposed a partition of the field into futuro-epistemology, whose aim was "to recognize objectively the future," and futuro-conceptionology, which was to be "futurology penetrated with the consciousness such as how the future should be or how the future could be planned."[46] In like manner, Fred Polak suggested futurography, to chart probable developments, and futopology, concerned with desirable developments.[47] No matter what the labels, these two sorts of forecasting deserve separate treatment.

FORECASTING THE VOLITIONAL SECTOR

Futurists are referring unrefelectingly to the volitional sector alone when they talk about shaping the future. And they speak of this all the time; the malleability of the future is one of the articles of faith in the field. Olaf Helmer, the deviser of several forecasting methods during his years with the Rand Corporation, proclaimed that "the future is so much more a matter of invention that of discovery";[48] Robert Theobald, no stranger to the counterculture, stated that "we make our own future";[49] for John Platt, situated ideologically somewhere between Helmer and Theobald, "the future lies open to our collective design and action."[50] Few futurists would care to disagree.

Forecasting in this sector is therefore done with the expectation that action is to be taken by those who intend to exert their will on the future, whether they be communards or corporate planners. "We want to forecast," de Jouvenel flatly stated, "in order to act."[51] In practice this often entails a reiterative process, beginning with a forecast of what might occur if no tinkering took place, followed by a trial plan, then a second forecast of the range of possible outcomes of the planning, then an improved plan, and so on until satisfaction results.[52] Government transportation officials might want first to project future highway needs, then plan for increased carrying capacity, then contemplate a picture of the future with all those roadways, then draw up alternative plans and study them, and so on.

An intriguing aspect of forecasting in this sector is that the importance of accuracy can be called into question. In Ulf Landergren's explanation of this curious point.

> For a "good" forecast about the influenceable environment it is of minor importance if "it comes true." The decision maker or planner will want to avoid or weaken forecasted "negative" trends and strengthen "positive" trends and will thus decide or plan so that the forecast does not "come true." The important thing is thus here if the forecast can be used in the decision or planning process.[53]

Truth is a poor criterion to look to in judging the worth of these forecasts because, first, accuracy cannot be ascertained without waiting long past the point where the forecasts would have some usefulness, and second, accuracy may have no chance of being realized if countervailing plans are adopted. A more utilitarian standard should be invoked instead. "A given set of predictions is better for us than another set if the future turns out to be more to our liking after we have been guided by this first set than it would have turned out had we been guided by the second set," proposed Fred Charles Ikle during the course of a close examination of these matters.[54]

It is in this sector, then, that forecasts can be contravened, and not only by planners. Public response to forecasts can work to nullify—or even enhance—what has been predicted. There is evidence, for example, that projections made in the 1950s concerning imminent shortages of scientists and engineers produced a change in enrollments in graduate schools of science and engineering that lead to surpluses.[55] Self-fulfilling and self-defying statements about the future are peculiar to this sector, and provision must be made for them.

In the way that forecasting the volitional sector is commonly practiced, McHale discovered, "major support in the field goes toward economic and technological forecasting."[56] These two aspects of the future have received the most attention partly because they are of great interest to the large-scale organizations which have the resources to commit to their study, and partly because they lend themselves to comparatively thorough-going and successful methods of exploration, since they are subject to quantification.

Economic forecasting, however, has in truth yet to be subsumed by futures research. While "the most obviously identifiable forerunner of the contemporary study of the future is economic forecasting,"[57] and while "the most sophisticated forecasting at present is done for short term changes in the economy,[58] Eldredge noted in 1972 that as of then there was little confluence of the "economic forecasting group" and the "growing future research stream."[59] A glance at what is presented at conferences and in the journals of futures research bears this out. Economic forecasters, the practitioners of a science of some standing, no doubt see little to be gained by joining forces with upstart futurists.

Technological forecasting, on the other hand, is unquestionably in the fold. Whether defined narrowly so as to refer only to the future of some technology,[60] or broadly so as to include other measurable concerns,[61] it involves the use of highly refined methods to create forecasts largely of the technical matters which are of interest to policy-makers, planners, and strategists. It is characterized less by the type of its subjects than by the rigor of its procedures. As some indication of the vitality of technological forecasting, it has been estimated that one hundred distinguishable techniques exist.[62] The origins of this variety of forecasting lie in military research and development,[63] but in recent years it has spread to private industry and the intellectual community at large.[64] Without doubt it constitutes the most vigorous segment of futures research.

FORECASTING THE NONVOLITIONAL SECTOR

When Daniel Bell said pithily, "It is the modern *hubris* that we can effect the conscious transformation of society,"[65] he was revealing a different view of the human enterprise than the one prevalent among those who forecast the volitional sector. As a sociologist Bell recognized how vast the realm is which lies beyond and impinges upon the area where choices can be made. This nonvolitional sector, massive and intractable, has order to it, and thus is in principle predictable.

Forecasting the nonvolitional sector represents an attempt to increase the scope of the science of forecasting—to take in more sweeping concerns and to probe further forward in time. Most of the work done in this vein falls under the rubric of "social forecasting," which is, in the definition by de Jouvenel that Hetman adopted for his dictionary, "the forecasting of big, slow changes in society."[66] The business of this branch of futures research, said Polak, "mainly consists of exploring and forecasting what presumably, at least with a high plausibility, might be bound to happen, if the autonomous forces now at work in social history . . . were going to proceed, with more or less impetus and impact, their rapid march towards the future."[67] "Socio-cultural forecasting" might be a more appropriate term, since these "big, slow changes," these "autonomous forces," involve not only social structures but also the behavioral patterns that determine a cultural milieu.

It should not be thought that such forecasting would have no utilitarian purpose. "The attainment of a broad perspective of impending change is of distinct aid in forecasting the particular," William Ogburn commonsensically pointed out a quarter-century ago at the dawn of futures research.[68] If anything this is even more true today, when social change is so profound that it can upset the best laid plans of government and industry. The vagaries of modern life compel technological forecasters to pay more and more attention to socio-cultural change.[69]

Despite the need, though, the state of socio-cultural forecasting is a sorry one. Duncan put the case succinctly: "A 'state of the art' report on social forecasting should, in all honesty, be quite brief. Such an art, in the sense of a coherent body of precepts and practices, has not yet been developed."[70] The sole exception, Duncan allowed, is demographic forecasting, which, for all its technique, has been remarkably unsuccessful.[71]

CONCLUSION

The future is conceived of as having two sectors: the first where volition may be employed to good effect, and the second containing all the human venture which is beyond deliberate manipulation. For forecasting these two sectors a new and robust science is rising, largely in response to the needs of decision-makers in modern large-scale organizations for information about the future.

Futures research, however, displays a lopsidedness in that forecasting the volitional sector is considerably advanced over forecasting the nonvolitional sector. This is reflected in McHale's finding that the personnel in the field is "heavily biased in the area of the physical sciences and engineering."[72] He goes on to say, "this type of professional training is not so directly sensitive to the evaluation of socio-cultural phenomena."[73] As a result, socio-cultural forecasting pales in comparison to technological forecasting.[74]

This deficiency deserves remedy:

> The curves of economic and technological forecasting do not yet take enough account of the species, which after all conceived these new methods of looking into the future. Unless we begin to devise some kind of "human forecasting," using the research done in such human sciences as sociology, psychology, anthropology, and philosophy, one essential part of futures research will be missing.[75]

Not only should the scope of futures research be widened to include the social environment, it should also be lengthened to longer terms, at least up to ten years. The thorough "Political and Economic Planning" (a British research group usually referred to as PEP) examination of futures research concluded by saying, "Two themes have run through this report: that there is an urgent need to think about the long-term future and that it is difficult to do so."[76]

The difficulty of forecasting the socio-cultural environment for a decade ahead can only be overcome through the development of new systematic methods. Such methods, if successful, would measurably increase the ability to plan, to protect, to confront the vicissitudes of these times—in short, to increase human mastery over what would otherwise be unmanageable circumstances.

On the way to devising one such method, it would be wise to recall de Jouvenel's advice: "To improve forecasting is to bring the intellectual process closer to the historical process."[77] If this can be taken as a motto, it may help keep the goal in sight and diminish the chances of going astray in the methodological byways which the intellect can turn up. The task is above all to approach the historical process.

A survey of social forecasting methods already in existence is an appropriate starting place.

NOTES

1. Kate Flores, " Step for Mankind," in Arthur Harkins, ed., *1971 American Anthropological Association Experimental Symposium on Cultural Futurology: Pre-Conference Volume* (Minneapolis: University of Minnesota, Office for Applied Social Science and the Future, 1971), F:24.

2. Otis Dudley Duncan, "Social Forecasting: The State of the Art," *The Public Interest* (Fall 1969), 17, 88.

3. Bertrand de Jouvenel, *Art of Conjecture*, trans. Nikita Lary (New York: Basic Books 1967), 6.

4. Edward S. Cornish, "President's Report," *The Futurist* (April 1973), VII:2, 85.

5. de Jouvenel, *Art of Conjecture*, 45.

6. Kenneth Boulding, *The Organizational Revolution* (New York: Harper & Bros., 1953, 4.

7. Ward Madden, "Forward," in Donald N. Michael, *The Unprepared Society: Planning for a Precarious Future* (New York: Basic Books, 1968), X.

8. Erich Jantsch, *Technological Forecasting in Perspective* (Paris: Organisation for Economic Cooperation and Development, 1967), 256.

9. Charles de Hoghton, William Page, and Guy Streatfeild, . . . *And Now the Future, A PEP Survey of Future Studies* (London: PEP, 1971), 63.

10. de Jouvenel, *Art of Conjecture*, 127.

11. Karl F. Schuessler, "Prediction," in David L. Sills, ed., *International Encyclopedia of the Social Sciences*, 17 vols. (New York: The Macmillan Co., 1968), XII: 423.

12. Eleanor Bernert Sheldon and Wilbert E. Moore, eds., *Indicators of Social Change* (New York: Russell Sage Foundation, 1968), 3.

13. Krishnan Kumar, "Inventing the Future in Spite of Futurology," *Futures* (December 1972), 4:4, 372.

14. Available in Ossip K. Flechtheim, *History and Futurology* (Meisenheim-am-Glan, Germany: Verlag Anton Hain, 1966), 64.

15. Alvin Toffler, ed., *The Futurists* (New York: Random House, 1972), 264.

16. "Discussion on Future Research," in Robert Jungk and Johan Galtung, eds., *Mankind 2000* (Oslo: Universitetsforlaget, 1969), 336.

17. Victor C. Ferkiss, *Technological Man: The Myth and the Reality* (New York: George Braziller, 1969), 12.

18. Bettina J. Huber and Wendell Bell, "Sociology and the Emergent Study of the Future,"*American Sociologist* (November 1971), 6:4, 287.

19. I.F. Clarke, "The Pattern of Prediction," *Futures* (September 1971), 3:3, 305.

20. Theodore J. Gordon, *The Current Methods of Futures Research* (Middletown, Conn.: The Institute for the Future, 1971), 2.

21. Wentworth Eldredge, "Teaching the Sociology of the Future, 1972," in Arthur M. Harkins, ed., *1972 American Sociological Association Seminar on the Sociology of the Future* (Minneapolis: University of Minnestoa, Office for Applied Social Science and the Future, 1972), E:3.

22. John McHale, *Typological Survey of Futures Research in the U.S.* (Binghamton, N.Y.: Center for Integrative Studies, 1970), 19.

23. Jantsch, *Technological Forecasting*, 271.

24. William H. Peterson, "The Future and the Futurists," *Harvard Business Review* (November-December, 1967), 45: 6, 185.

25. Jantsch, *Technological Forecasting*, 106.

26. de Jouvenel, *Art of Conjecture*, 17.

27. Ibid., 18.

28. Herman Kahn and B. Bruce-Briggs, *Things to Come* (New York: The Macmillan Co., 1972), 1.

29. Alvin Toffler, *Future Shock* (New York: Random House, 1970), 407.

30. Fred L. Polak, *Prognostics* (New York: Elsevier, 1970).

31. McHale, *Typological Survey*, 6.

32. Edward S. Cornish, "The Professional Futurist," in Jungk and Galtung, eds., 245.

33. McHale, *Typological Survey*, 8.

34. Igor V. Bestuzhev-Lada, "A Soviet Scientist Looks at Futurology," *The UNESCO Courier* (April 1971), 24.

35. de Hoghton et al., *Now the Future*, 33.

36. "Discussion," 337.

37. Yujiro Hayashi, "The Direction and Orientation of Futurology as a Science," in Jungk and Galtung, eds., 270.

38. Henri Bergson, *Time and Free Will*, trans. F. L. Pogson (New York: The Macmillan Co., 1910), 10.

39. de Jouvenel, *Art of Conjecture*, 17.

40. Schuessler, "Prediction," 418.

41. Wilbert E. Moore, "Forecasting the Future: The United States in 1980," *The Educational Record* (Fall 1964), 45:4, 342.

42. Jantsch, *Technological Forecasting*, 15.

43. Paul Dickson, *Think Tanks* (New York: Ballantine Books, 1971), 326.

44. Albert Wilson and Donna Wilson, "Toward the Institutionalization of Change," in Magoroh Maruyama, ed., *1970 American Anthropological Association Cultural Futurology Symposium: Pre-Conference Volume* (Minneapolis: University of Minnesota, 1970), 12:5.

45. Robert Theobald, Alternative Methods of Predicting the Future," *The Futurist* (April 1969), III:2, 45.

46. Hayashi, "Futurology as a Science," 270.

47. Polak, *Prognostics*, 306.

48. Olaf Helmer, *On the Future State of the Union* (Menlo Park, Calif.: Institute for the Future, 1972), 71.

49. Theobald, "Alternative Methods," 45.

50. John Platt, "How Men Can Shape Their Future," *Futures* (March 1971), 3:1, 47.

51. de Jouvenel, *Art of Conjecture*, 113.

52. Ibid., 54.

53. Ulf Landergren, "Forecasting as an Aid to Planning—A Few Concepts," in Japan Society of Futurology, comp., *Challenges from the Future*, 3 vols. (Tokyo: Kodansha, 1970), I, 281.

54. Fred Charles Ikle, "Can Social Predictions Be Evaluated?" in Daniel Bell, ed., *Toward the Year 2000: Work in Progress* (Boston: Beacon Press, 1967), 112.

55. Donald A. Schon, "Forecasting and Technological Forecasting," in Bell, ed., *Toward the Year 2000*, 136.

56. McHale, *Typological Survey*, 25.

57. de Hoghton et al., *Now the Future*, 8.

58. Bertrand de Jouvenel, "Notes on Social Forecasting," in Michael Young, ed., *Forecasting and the Social Sciences* (London: Social Science Research Council, 1968), 119.

59. Eldredge, "Sociology of the Future," E:4.

60. Schon, "Forecasting and Technological Forecasting," 127.

61. Dickson, *Think Tanks*, 328.

62. Jantsch, *Technological Forecasting*, 113.

63. Robert U. Ayres, *Technological Forecasting and Long-Range Planning* (New York: McGraw-Hill, 1969).

64. Schon, "Forecasting and Technological Forecasting," 127.

65. Daniel Bell, "Twelve Modes of Prediction—A Preliminary Sorting of

Approaches in the Social Sciences," *Daedalus* (Summer 1964), 93:2, 846.

66. de Jouvenel, *Art of Conjecture,* 240; François Hetman, *The Language of Forecasting* (Paris: Futuribles, 1969), 346.

67. Fred L. Polak, "Toward the Goals of Goals," in Jungk and Galtung, eds., 322.

68. William Fielding Ogburn, with the assistance of Jean L. Adams and S. C. Gilfillan, *The Social Effects of Aviation* (Boston: Houghton-Mifflin, 1946), 56.

69. James R. Bright, *A Brief Introduction to Technology Forecasting* (Austin, Texas: The Pemaquid Press, 1972), 3:5.

70. Duncan, "Social Forecasting," 88.

71. Ibid., 93.

72. McHale, *Typological Survey,* 42.

73. Ibid.

74. Radovan Richta and Ota Sulc, "Forecasting and the Scientific and Technological Revolution," *International Social Science Journal* (November 1969), XXI:4, 571.

75. Robert Jungk, "Human Futures," *Futures* (September 1968), 1:1, 34.

76. de Hoghton et al., *Now the Future,* 63.

77. de Jouvenel, *Art of Conjecture,* 60.

CHAPTER 2

Methods of social forecasting: extrapolation from social systems

THE TWO MODES OF SOCIO-CULTURAL FORECASTING

What methods there are for the systematic forecasting of the "big, slow changes in society" that describe the nonvolitional social future derive from two approaches. The first is to project forward an understanding of the social system in question; the second is to predict from a knowledge of members' attitudes which are alleged to direct those systems. The culture-wide psychological elements (such as a people's values) which are the essentials of this second group of methods will be examined in the following chapter.

Here, the first group is the subject—the ways of extrapolating from social systems themselves. Focus is not upon the collective outlooks of their members, but upon the ongoing dynamics which define the systems they are immersed in. "Every social group constitutes a system; it is a tautology that the future states of a system can be known if its dynamics are completely known."[1] Since such dynamics remain stubbornly obscure, the methods in this group are less than perfect.

One subdivision of this approach is represented by the accretion in the sociological tradition over the past 150 years. The other consists of methods which have issued from operations research and systems analysis since World War II. Most of this latter methodological undertaking occurred at the Rand Corporation, the most famous of the American institutions known as "think tanks."

But before turning to the methods of social system forecasting found inside and outside sociology, there is one procedure common to all the corners of futures research, and it gets mention first. This is the use of trend measurements.

SOCIAL TRENDS

A trend is the most readily understood means of extending a present awareness into the future unknown. It is by nature unadorned and certainly directional. There is no elaborate conceptual framework to be mastered, nor is it difficult to determine the likely range, albeit widening in time, of future quantities. All that has to be done is to take some matter of interest—population, or divorce rates, or the incidence of hat-wearing—and establish a measure, gather data for a time series, and finally project the curve ahead. The underlying premise of this sort of forecasting is "that the combined effect of internal and external factors which produced a trend over a past period will remain the same during a future one."[2] Schuessler summarized the attributes of trends when he spoke of "the process of predicting a variable from itself."[3]

Many futurists have found this to be an adequate method of socio-cultural forecasting. The Wilsons (calling the nonvolitional sector "the determinative") wrote:

> The primary problem of the determinative in futures research is to discover the basic patterns of social change and use these patterns to forecast the most probable future states of society that will develop accordingly. The primary methodology of the determinative is the extrapolation into the future of the magnitudes of quantitative statistical time series that have

been derived by fitting to past quantities. The trends indicated
by these series are our best guides to the most probably determinative futures since technological, ecological, or social
trends seldom change direction rapidly.[4]

In their view the inertia of the social environment is sufficient to
permit this procedure.

Currently the most concerted effort at the collection of social
trend data is carried on in what is known as "the social indicator
movement"—"movement" no doubt because of its quick growth
and moralistic aspect. Precursors of the movement go back to 1929,
when President Hoover established a commission to survey changes
in American life. The commission's report, which came out in 1933,
covered such topics as social attitudes, rural life, the family, recreation and leisure time activities, crime and punishment, population,
and government.[5] Renewed interest in quantifying social phenomena came to the fore in the 1960s as a result of the federal government's need for better information to be employed in the planning
process. This need was fully pointed up in the report of President
Eisenhower's Commission on National Goals.[6] the name being indicative of the normative orientation of these social statistics. By
the time the Johnson administration's *Toward a Social Report* was
published in 1969 (concerned with goal areas of health, opportunity, environment, standards of living, learning, and democratic
values),[7] interest in social indicators had spread far beyond government circles. Raymond Bauer's influential book, *Social Indicators*,
had appeared in 1966,[8] followed by Eleanor Bernert Sheldon's and
Wilbert Moore's *Indicators of Social Change* in 1968[9] and Bertram
Gross's *Social Intelligence for America's Future* in 1969.[10]

Social indicators, then, are not measures of just any social trends,
but of those which relate to objectives.[11] Bauer, who is usually
among the least sentimental of social scientists, said that they "enable us to assess where we stand and are going with respect to our
values and goals."[12] It is this pious quality of the social indicator
movement which Eleanor Sheldon and Howard Freeman have felt
called upon to censure in the interest of better research,[13] but apparently there is no getting away from it.

The irrepressible tendentiousness of human beings, social scientists included, may explain why some social indicators are such poor measures of the trends they pretend to capture. "Virtually every trend series pertaining to social problems has a built-in inflationary bias that would make it look as though things were 'getting worse,' unless the trend for improvement were very strong," maintained Bauer.[14] Rising mental illness statistics reflect social changes other than rising mental illness;[15] traffic safety figures are actually improving, contrary to impressions;[16] crime rates can go up as a function of inflation, not crime.[17] The latter deception results in part from the improper fusion of several subindicators into one index; the opposite error, of making excessive use of one indicator alone, is also common.[18]

But the problems with social indicators extend beyond their accuracy in collection and formulation—which probably could be corrected—to their relationship with theory.

> The lack of theoretical orientation is perhaps the most basic criticism and also the most obvious need of the social indicator movement. Concepts need to be identified in some taxonomical format with further explication of sub-concepts and their operationalization. Thus far, the accomplishments in these areas have been less than adequate.[19]

There is no escaping the fact that forecasting by means of trends, minus theory, is profoundly naive in principle. "Prediction by trends gives us a view of the world as if it were a handful of sand, each particle distinct from the others."[20] Only ignorance of related factors could lead one to say that rising population numbers will have no top or the declining hat market no bottom. More credible forecasts would logically result from a knowledge of contingent matters. As Michael Young put it, "The more that past and present interrelationships are understood, the more discriminate their extension."[21]

The attempts to articulate social change and produce discriminating projections have been weightily theoretical on the part of sociologists and adventurously atheoretical for others. Each campaign has, in its way, fallen short.

SOCIAL SYSTEM EXTRAPOLATION
WITHIN SOCIOLOGY

Although founded in the nineteenth century as the previsionary social science, sociology has never come to embrace the study of the future.[22] Sociologists have increasingly found it prudent to limit, rather than add to, the number of intangibles from which they must make sense;[23] in recognition of the immensity of their subject, this is only reasonable. The result is that when they study social change—a topic never quite in fashion[24]—they do so with hardly a thought for prediction. The emphasis has been on explaining change through the past, instead of on anticipating change in the future.

Not only has the study of social change been almost exclusively historical, but also the level of analysis has consistently been too abstract to permit the derivation of socio-cultural forecasting procedures for a mere decade ahead. The theories generated often have a time range of millennia and often reduce the complications of social change to one or two grand variables. In their expansiveness they are essentially untestable and unusable. These are the theories which Wilbert Moore, onetime president of the American Sociological Association, said "explain too little because they attempt too much."[25]

One class of sociological analyses does appear especially productive, however, if only because of its generic caution. "Modernization theories" argue that societies which are industrializing will pass through a series of discernible transformations.[26] Broadly speaking, these states relate to the increasing differentiation and specialization of roles, the growth of technologized economies, the development of populistic sentiments, and the dislocation which must accompany such changes.[27] Refinements in these theories may eventually permit deft, precise forecasting. Moore called these "recapitulated experiences" a sound basis for prediction,[28] and clearly they are—if one is interested in the followers rather than the leaders. But to determine the direction of the leading edge of social change, other methods would be necessary.

This problem has been addressed sporadically in the history of sociology. The course of societies, indeed, of civilizations, was the

subject of so-called rise-and-fall theorists, who include Oswald
Spengler, Arnold Toynbee, and Pitirim Sorokin. Among futurists
Sorokin's name is the most often heard nowadays, largely because
Herman Kahn credited Sorokin with discerning the major trend of
modern life, the trend toward "sensate" culture (empirical, secular,
epicurean—in short, based on the premise that sensation validates
belief).[29] Curiously Sorokin's own prediction was just the opposite, of decreasing "sensate" culture, and increasing "ideational"
culture (one based on the premise that supernatural forces validate
belief), or possibly "idealistic" culture (a combination of the other
two).[30] In any event, in Daniel Bell's summary of forecasing methods,
all such rhythmic theories were discounted because they can not be
verified.[31] Moore, too, leveled the standard criticism: "Such sweeping views are likely to be more useful as literary devices than as
scientific representations of change."[32]

A steadier conception of social change distinguished evolutionary
theorists, best represented by Herbert Spencer (and anticipated in
some respects by Auguste Comte). In the wake of Charles Darwin's
explanation of natural evolution, these thinkers held that social
evolution was toward ever greater complexity and integration.[33]
Evolutionary theories shared in the assumption that such movement signals progress or betterment.[34] Like rise-and-fall theories,
however, they provided so general a gloss that in detail they could
neither describe[35] nor predict.[36]

If the evolutionary theory were correct in every instance, the
work of Burnham Putnam Beckwith would be vastly superior to his
nineteenth-century predecessors. Beckwith too saw an irrevocable
advance in store for mankind as the successes of industrial societies
became universal.[37] This sort of eternal linearity, true or not, does
all too little to explain the modulations of the socio-cultural environment from decade to decade.

A more sophisticated analysis would be promised with bivariate
schemes; if an independent variable could be found, then its modi-
fication would predict other social changes. This search began in
earnest with Karl Marx, who thought that varying modes of production were the key to understanding how historical change took
place.[38] Changes in the mode of production preceded changes in the

organization of production and of society. Specifically, Marx felt that the excesses of industrialization foretold the imminent uprising of workers, leading to the establishment of a society which lacked classes. Needless to say, it has not turned out this way; it was the societies most exposed to industrialization which avoided class warfare, and some of the less industrialized which suffered it. Industrialization is a poor augury of communism. The result has been to cast Marx's vast intellectual apparatus into doubt. Its capacity to predict is now widely admitted to be small.[39]

Yet those who came after Marx and continued his hunt for the major variable in the fluctuation of human systems owed much to his materialistic view. Important among them was William Fielding Ogburn, who affirmed that Marxist thought formed the groundwork for his theory of cultural lag.[40] Ogburn's theory has been described as "the proposition that technological trends of the past provide a useful key to cultural trends of the future,"[41] a position that Ogburn himself sometimes promoted without reservation,[42] and sometimes found too narrow.[43] In any case, the technological determinism with which he is commonly bracketed has much to recommend it as a basis for prediction, and many futurists have pledged themselves to it.[44] The scope is finite enough; reasonable hypotheses could be formulated, on the order of this technology having that effect; measurement would seem to be possible.

Unfortunately, Ogburn's theory has borne little fruit. The relationship between technology and social change is much more intricate than Ogburn suggested (which may explain why the final report of Harvard University's Program on Technology and Society could not be more informative[45]). First, not all technologies, once developed, get adopted; it has been pointed out that "modern society 'selects' its technology from a universe of alternative possibilities."[46] It selects some, as television, and rejects others, as the video-phone, for reasons that are not fully comprehended. And even if a technology is selected, and does begin to influence social change, its continued influence is not guaranteed, for it can later be discarded, as is happening with the telegraph.

Assuming that a technology is one which will become tightly integrated into social systems, its future effects are still near-impossible to describe, Peter Drucker has argued with conviction.[47] DDT was originally synthesized for use on humans as a mild insecticide; no one foresaw that its use would extend to crops, forests, or livestock, would sully the natural environment, or would precipitate a massive public reaction. Computers were predicted to be of use for military and scientific purposes, but not in business or government. The best market forecasts of the early 1950s saw a mere 1,000 computers in existence by the year 2000. Automation, which was supposed to eradicate middle management, lead to its growth. Concluded Drucker, "The future impact of technology is almost always beyond anyone's imagination."[48]

The quest for the lever of social change subsequently turned to a more rarefied tool—knowledge itself. The thesis of Daniel Bell, the contemporary sociologist most closely identified with the study of the future, was that

the major source of structural change in society—the change in the modes of innovation in the relation of science to technology and in public policy—is the change in the character of knowledge: the exponential growth and branching of science, the rise of a new intellectual technology, the creation of systematic research through R & D budgets, and, as the calyx of all this, the codification of theoretical knowledge.[49]

From this will issue "post-industrial society":

A post-industrial society is based on services. Hence, it is a game between persons. What counts is not raw muscle power, or energy, but information. The central person is the professional, for he is equipped, by his education and training, to provide the kinds of skill which are increasingly demanded in the post-industrial society. If an industrial society is defined by the quantity of goods as marking a standard of living, the post-industrial society is defined by the quality of life as measured by services and amenities—health, education, recreation, and the arts—which are now deemed desirable and possible for everyone.[50]

For the educated this is a particularly pleasing view of the future, if not a sop for their recurrent powerlessness in history. But like the theories of the earlier social philosophers, it presents too broad a conception of social change to generate forecasting procedures for the limited time span that must concern most futurists. Once again, utility is lost to grandeur.

This is also the charge against Marshall McLuhan, who, although not ordinarily thought of as a sociologist, offered up a theory of social change which was not the intellectual inferior of Ogburn's or Bell's, or perhaps even Marx's. His variable (taken over from the work of his fellow Canadian, Harold Innis) was the changing means of communication, quite apart from what is expressly conveyed.[51] McLuhan asserted that the massive alterations wreaked on Western civilization by the arrival of print were going to be matched by what the electronic media were accomplishing. These notions of McLuhan are at once intriguing to the point of acceptance, vague to the point of dismissal.

Thus both the univariate and bivariate schemes have been unsatisfactory devices for prediction. The conclusion of Otis Dudley Duncan's survey of sociological forecasting methods was that Ogburn's cultural lag theory represented the high water mark, such as it was.[52] Nor does there seem to be much chance of improvement. "Basic research into social structure and process is not, it can be suggested, making satisfactory progress," said C.E. Lindblom in response to a call for predictive sociology.[53] Those who foresee the rise of a prognostic subdiscipline within the field[54] may be expressing unreasonable hopes—a tendency of futurists. Stuck at the problem of explanation, and with the static conception of human systems which that can impose,[55] sociology is a long way from commitment to prediction.

SOCIAL SYSTEM EXTRAPOLATION
OUTSIDE SOCIOLOGY

In recent years a comparatively more vigorous effort at the development of social forecasting methods has been undertaken by people trained not in sociology, but in fields which were tapped for operations researchers and systems analysts. Due to the great need of their organizations to recognize the future, they were compelled to venture where sociologists were reluctant to. Although one of the best-regarded of their number referred to their achievements as "rudimentary devices,"[56] the procedures they devised still constitute a methodological gain for futures research.

Robert Nisbet was being misleading when he said, "It would be really a shabby trick if we somehow left the inference around, to be picked up by the public, that computers and systems-analysts do look into the future in ways that were denied to a Tocqueville or a Marx."[57] The new methods have scientific and utilitarian pretensions that were foreign to earlier social philosophers. Without question they provide more rational, more relevant aid for policy formulation. (In fact, to serve decision-makers, they were designed with the volitional sector in mind; but since they are also used to delve into the nonvolitional sector, they are discussed here.)

Herman Kahn, a physicist by education, is perhaps the most famous of the futurists to come from the Rand Corporation, where many of these methods originated. The technique most frequently linked with Kahn is the writing of scenarios.[58] "A scenario, or 'future history,' is a narrative description of a potential course of developments which might lead to some future state of affairs," explained Theodore Gordon in his review of nonsociological methods in futures research.[59] To Kahn, the purpose of scenarios was to display, in as dramatic and persuasive a fashion as possible, a number of possibilities for the future.[60] One, for instance, depicted a worldwide depression commencing in the late 1970s:

> In the developing countries, economies are devastated. Their currency reserves are wiped out and their export markets nearly disappear. Unilateral aid is abandoned and the IBRD and other development banks are handicapped by defaulting creditors and inability to market new bond issues. Development plans are scrapped and governments fall. They are replaced with indigenous forms of state socialism ostensibly dedicated to equitable income distribution but often really pursuing forms of state capitalism and rigorously surpressing

dissent. By and large the history of the Russian and Chinese revolutions is repeated. The new regimes seek to develop in largely closed economics with some technical assistance, little trade, and no outside capital. By the turn of the century a few of the best endowed of the developing countries have reachieved the level of GNP they had reached in the late 1970's, and the growth rates of the highly industrialized countries, after a long period of stagnation, begin to turn up again.[61]

By Kahn's own admission, however, the scenario was not a predictive instrument in and of itself;[62] there was no explanatory component, no evaluatory procedure. At bottom it relied on nothing more than intuition and theatricality. As such, its only function can be "to 'sensitize' both its author and his readers to the possibility of alternative futures and the wide range of factors that can or might influence these futures."[63]

Another Rand alumnus, less of a public figure but more of a methodologist, is the mathematician Olaf Helmer. Helmer recognized, perhaps more deeply than others, the dimensions of the problems in the study of change, and in 1959 coauthored a paper which argued ingeniously for the uncoupling of prediction from explanation in the inexact sciences, foremost among them the study of social systems.[64] He felt that "once the common belief in the identity of predictive and explanatory scientific procedures is seen to be incorrect, it is clearly appropriate to consider the nature and potentialities of predictive procedures distinct from those used for explanation."[65] The two predictive procedures he had in mind, further detailed in his subsequent book *Social Technology*, were the polling of experts (the "Delphi technique," as it has come to be called), and the construction of models.[66]

In Helmer's words, "Delphi is a systematic method of collecting opinions from a group of experts through a series of questionnaires, in which feedback of the group's opinion distribution is provided between question rounds while preserving the anonymity of the responses."[67] By keeping the experts apart, it was thought that the worst aspects of group interaction would be avoided, and the collective wisdom would emerge untrammeled. Over the course of several rounds, the panelists' predictions (which are usually stated as probabilities on a time scale, in reply to specific questions) were bound to converge, and a consensus forecast result.

The technique has proved to be attractive and has been used hundreds of times since its first large-scale trial in 1964.[68] Occasionally it has been applied to the nonvolitional sector, although Helmer has been careful to point out that less is to be expected from social forecasts than from technological forecasts.[69] In 1970 Helmer and Raul de Brigard issued their study entitled *Some Potential Societal Developments 1970-2000*, which made use of a thirty-four member panel to explore twelve social areas, including urbanization, the family, leisure, and values.[70] Generally speaking, the results were melioristic: "The panel of respondents in this study looked upon the development of new analytical tools and institutional reforms as providing society with the prospects of synthesis of power and knowledge that might permit it to be governed effectively in terms of social as well as economic priorities."[71] A similar but smaller Delphi, with seven in-house participants, was reported in Helmer's book *On the Future State of the Union*.[72] Less optimistic views of the social future were turned out from another one conducted in 1973.[73]

The accuracy and procedures of the Delphi technique have yet to be thoroughly investigated,[74] but there is some favorable evidence: one study indicated that different panels produce similar forecasts;[75] another, quoted by Gordon, found the Delphi procedure to be more exact than other methods for short-term economic forecasts;[76] a third reported that for the original 1964 Delphi forecasts, fifteen of the twenty-two events predicted to occur before 1970 did in fact take place.[77]

Yet the Delphi technique will always be vulnerable to charges that it operates without theory or data, and that its protocols produce consensus forecasts irrespective of historical truth.[78] Since no premium is placed on anything more reasoned, the initial predictions of the panelists are conjectures of the most primitive sort, atheoretical and subjective. The bases for prediction—the participants' private conceptualizations of social change—go unexamined, to the impairment of the quality of the projections. Agreement is then reached not through a comparison of rationales, but through whatever the personality factors are which cause one sort of individual to hold his ground and and another to compromise. In view of all this, Daniel Bell urged moving on to another technique:

> In short, if forecasting is to advance, it has to be within a sys-tem context which specifies the major social, political, and economic relationships that will obtain at any given time. In the RAND use of the Delphi technique, what we are given is a set of possibilities, but the way in which these possibilities are combined depends upon the system in which they are embedded. And the art—or science—of forecasting can be extended only when we are able to advance the creation of models of the social system itself.[79]

Indeed, models were Helmer's other suggested method. In partic-ular, a simulation model is one designed to imitate, in an approxi-mate fashion, the time-varying features of complex systems.[80] The immensity of the task warrants the use of computers, which im-poses the requirement that the model be mathematically stated. "The importance of formal models lies in their ability to contain more complex relationships than can be comprehended by the unaided intellect," noted Klaus Lompe, who then called attention to their chief limitation: "one must realize that such constructions mostly contain inadmissible simplifications and can only give very re-stricked information about the real processes going on."[81]

The most ambitious simulation model so far, which appeared as a Club of Rome report entitled *The Limits to Growth*,[82] was fabri-cated by students of MIT's Jay W. Forrester, a pioneer in computer technology and in the modeling of business sytems. The five varia-bles chosen by the modelers were population growth, resource de-pletion, food supply, capital investment, and pollution. Strikingly, the model forecasted calamity within a century if the variables continued their present arrangements and courses.[83]

A thorough-going critique of the model has been prepared by the Science Policy Research Unit of the University of Sussex in the United Kingdom.[84] As they reminded their readers at the outset, "Any model of any social system necessarily involves assumptions about the workings of that system, and these assumptions are nec-essarily coloured by the attitudes and values of the group concerned"[85]

The fallacious assumptions of Forrester's students, they claimed, devolved from the naive acceptance of neo-Malthusian positions. If only the modelers had included a variable of technical progress; it "has the effect of indefinitely postponing the catastrophes which the model otherwise predicts."[86]

Despite whatever flawed content the *Limits to Growth* model may contain, the elegance and power of the method is undeniable. It is from simulations like this one that futurists draw hope: "the simulations models will be the most important tools of coming futurology—the tools with the highest predictive power"[87] is a typical reflection. And yet, as the Sussex team deflatingly remarked, "Computer models cannot replace theory."[88] Simulations carry out the implications of what has been supposed about a social system, so advances in modeling must await advances in theorizing.

Meanwhile, other less costly techniques are also receiving their share of attention. A frequently mentioned one is cross-impact analysis, "an experimental approach by which the probability of each item in a forecasted set can be adjusted in view of judgments relative to potential interactions of the forecasted items."[89] Specified events (such as a revolutionary attempt to overthrow a government) and trends (the rise in per capita GNP, for instance) are set up in a grid, and the chances and results of their interaction are estimated. With the aid of a computer, the values of each cell are adjusted until the overall matrix provides a coherent picture of future possibilities. But like Delphis and simulations, quasi-models such as a cross-impact analysis also operate on unproven notions about the nature of society.

CONCLUSION

With regard to social systems, Wilbert Moore remarked, "Uncertainty and lack of precise predictability arise from the complexity of dynamic factors—that is, from a rather large error factor owing to the number and interplay of uncontrolled variables,"[90] and so indicated what all those who would develop socio-cultural forecasting methods must constantly confront—how forbidding the subject matter is. The awesomely intricate workings of social systems render informed and accurate projection near impossible.

The complex interactions which characterize all but most trivial instances of social behavior, the interplay of biological, psychological, and cultural determinants of that behavior, our inability to identify, isolate, and measure the effects of even the major factors among these determinants, and the halo of indeterminacy surrounding even the most straightforward measures and indices of social behavior or characteristics, all of these limitations effectively guarantee that any generalizations arrived at are either sufficiently abstract as to have little explanatory or predictive significance, or so specified and qualified as to apply only over a highly restricted domain.[91]

The attempt to generate productive conceptual schemes within the discipline of sociology has been halting; the attempt to venture on without them has been brave but at root eminently suspect. Looking over the social forecasting procedures both inside and outside sociology, Daniel Bell was forced to conclude how unavailing the intellectual expense had been.[92]

But a way around this methodological predicament has been proposed. It is to give short shrift to the dynamics of a social system and instead to examine those attitudes that provide guidance for a person's behavior, in the belief that if they guide the individual and guide multitudes of individuals, then they guide society. In theory, a knowledge of these attitudes would have considerable predictive value and would serve as a great expedient in the forecasting of the nonvolitional sector.

NOTES

1. Bertrand de Jouvenel, *Art of Conjecture*, trans. Nikita Lary (New York: Basic Books, 1967), 74.

2. Erich Jantsch, *Technological Forecasting in Perspective* (Paris: Organisation for Economic Cooperation and Development, 1967), 156.

3. Karl F. Schuessler, "Prediction," in David L. Sills, ed., *International Encyclopedia of the Social Sciences*, 17 vols. (New York: The Macmillan Co., 1968), XII, 420.

4. Albert Wilson and Donna Wilson, "Toward the Institutionalization

of Change," in Magoroh Maruyama, ed., *1970 American Anthropological Association Cultural Futurology Symposium: Pre-Conference Volume* (Minneapolis: University of Minnesota, 1970), 12:6.

5. President's Research Committee on Social Trends, *Recent Social Trends* (New York: McGraw-Hill, 1933).

6. President's Commission on National Goals, *Goals for Americans: Programs for Action in the Sixties* (Englewood Cliffs, N.J.: Prentice-Hall, 1960).

7. U.S. Department of Health, Education, and Welfare, *Toward a Social Report* (Washington, D.C.: U.S. Government Printing Office, 1969).

8. Raymond A. Bauer, ed., *Social Indicators* (Cambridge, Mass., The MIT Press, 1966).

9. Eleanor Bernert Sheldon and Wilbert E. Moore, eds., *Indicators of Social Change* (New York: Russell Sage Foundation, 1968).

10. Bertram M. Gross, ed., *Social Intelligence for America's Future* (Boston: Allyn & Bacon, 1969).

11. U.S. Department of Health, Education, and Welfare, *Social Report*, 97.

12. Raymond A. Bauer, "Detection and Anticipation of Impact: The Nature of the Task," in Bauer, ed., *Social Indicators*, 27.

13. Eleanor Bernert Sheldon and Howard E. Freeman, "Notes on Social Indicators: Promises and Potential," *Policy Sciences* (April 1970), 1:1, 98.

14. Bauer, "Detection," 27.

15. Ibid.

16. Ibid., 29.

17. Ibid., 30.

18. Amitai Etzioni and Edward W. Lehman, "Some Dangers in 'Valid' Social Measurement," in Gross, ed., *Social Intelligence*, 48.

19. Ralph M. Brooks, "Social Planning and Societal Monitoring," in Leslie D. Wilcox, Ralph M. Brooks, George M. Beal, Gerald E. Klonglan, eds., *Social Indicators and Societal Monitoring* (San Francisco: Jossey-Bass, 1972), 10.

20. "The Nature and Limitation of Forecasting," in Daniel Bell, ed., *Toward the Year 2000: Work in Progress* (Boston: Beacon Press, 1967), 331.

21. Michael Young, "Forecasting and the Social Sciences," in Michael Young, ed., *Forecasting and the Social Sciences* (London: Social Science Research Council, 1963), 15.

22. John McHale, *The Future of the Future* (New York: Ballantine Books, 1971), 277.

23. Henry Winthrop, "The Sociologist and the Study of the Future," *The American Sociologist* (May 1968), 3:2, 141.

24. Sheldon and Moore, *Social Change*, 5.

25. Wilbert E. Moore, "A Reconsideration of Theories of Social Change," *American Sociological Review* (December 1960), 25:6, 811.

26. Richard Appelbaum, *Theories of Social Change* (Chicago: Markham Publishing Co., 1970), 36.

27. S.N. Eisenstadt, *Modernization: Protest and Change* (Englewood Cliffs, N.J.: Prentice-Hall, 1966), 2-4.

28. Wilbert E. Moore, "Forecasting the Future: The United States in 1980," *The Educational Record* (Fall, 1964), 45:4, 342.

29. Herman Kahn and Anthony J. Wiener, *The Year 2000* (New York: The Macmillan Co., 1967), 7.

30. Pitirim Sorokin, *Social and Cultural Dynamics* (Boston: Porter Sargent, 1957), 703.

31. Daniel Bell, "Twelve Modes of Prediction—A Preliminary Sorting of Approaches in the Social Sciences," *Daedalus* (Summer 1964), 93:2, 847.

32. Wilbert E. Moore, *Social Change* (Englewood Cliffs, N.J.: Prentice-Hall, 1963), 36.

33. Appelbaum, *Social Change*, 30.

34. Amitai Etzioni and Eva Etzioni, eds., *Social Change* (New York: Basic Books, 1964), 80.

35. Appelbaum, *Social Change*, 130.

36. Sheldon and Moore, *Social Change*, 6.

37. Burnham Putnam Beckwith, *The Next 500 Years: Scientific Predictions of Major Social Trends* (New York: Exposition Press, 1967), 11.

38. Karl Marx, *A Contribution to the Critique of Political Economy*, trans. N. I. Stone (Chicago: Charles H. Kerr & Co., 1904), 11.

39. Sheldon and Moore, *Social Change*, 6.

40. William F. Ogburn, *On Culture and Social Change*, ed. and with an introduction by Otis Dudley Duncan (Chicago: University of Chicago Press, 1964), 87.

41. Schuessler, "Prediction," 419.

42. Ogburn, *Culture and Social Change*, 85.

43. Ibid., 92.

44. Victor C. Ferkiss, *Technological Man: The Myth and the Reality* (New York: George Braziler, 1969), 14.

45. Harvard University Program on Technology and Society, *A Final Review* (Cambridge, Mass.: Harvard University, 1972).

46. Sheldon and Moore, *Social Change*, 7.

47. Peter F. Drucker, "New Technology," *The New York Times* (April 8, 1973).

48. Ibid., 1.

49. Daniel Bell, *The Coming of the Post-Industrial Society* (New York: Basic Books, 1973), 44.

50. Ibid., 127.

51. Marshall McLuhan, *Understanding Media: The Extensions of Man* (New York: New American Library 1964), 24.

52. Otis Dudley Duncan, "Social Forecasting: The State of the Art," *The Public Interest* (Fall 1969), 17, 106.

53. C. E. Lindblom, "Comments on Simon," in William R. Ewald, ed., *Environment and Policy: The Next 50 Years* (Bloomington: Indiana University Press, 1968), 385.

54. Bettina J. Huber and Wendell Bell, "Sociology and the Emergent Study of the Future," *American Sociologist* (November 1971), 6:4, 293.

55. Wilbert E. Moore, "The Utility of Utopias," *American Sociological Review* (December 1966), 31:6, 766.

56. Olaf Helmer, *On the Future State of the Union* (Menlo Park, Calif.: The Institute for the Future, 1972), 112.

57. Robert A. Nisbet, "The Year 2000 and All That," *Commentary* (June 1968), 45:6, 62.

58. Bell, "Twelve Modes of Prediction," 865.

59. Theodore J. Gordon, *The Current Methods of Futures Research* (Middletown, Conn.: The Institute for the Future, 1971), 31.

60. Kahn and Wiener, *Year 2000,* 263.

61. Ibid., 336.

62. Ibid., 264.

63. Charles de Hoghton, William Page, and Guy Streatfeild, . . . *And Now the Future. A PEP Survey of Future Studies* (London: PEP, 1971), 56.

64. Olaf Helmer and Nicholas Rescher, "On the Epistemology of the Inexact Sciences," *Management Science* (October 1959), 6:1, 25-52.

65. Ibid., 51.

66. Olaf Helmer, with contributions by Bernice Brown and Theodore Gordon, *Social Technology* (New York: Basic Books, 1966).

67. Helmer, *Future State of the Union,* 15.

68. Gordon, *Methods of Futures Research,* 13.

69. Helmer, *Future State of the Union,* 22.

70. Olaf Helmer and Raul de Brigard, *Some Potential Societal Developments 1970-2000* (Middletown, Conn.: The Institute for the Future, 1970).

71. Ibid., 123.

72. Helmer, *Future State of the Union,* 30-42.

73. "Pessimistic View of Future Issued," *The New York Times* (September 24, 1973).

74. Fritz R. S. Dressler, "Subjective Methodology in Forecasting," *Technological Forecasting and Social Change* (1972), 3:4, 433.

75. Joseph Martino, "The Consistency of Delphi Forecasts," *The Futurist* (April 1970), IV:2, 64.

76. Gordon, *Methods of Futures Research*, 15.

77. Robert H. Ament, "Comparison of Delphi Forecasting Studies in 1964 and 1967," *Futures* (March 1970), II:1, 17.

78. W. Timothy Weaver, "The Delphi Forecasting Method," *Phi Delta Kappan* (January 1971), LII:1, 268.

79. Daniel Bell, "The Measurement of Knowledge and Technology," in Sheldon and Moore, eds., 192.

80. Gordon, *Methods of Futures Research*, 21.

81. Klaus Lompe, "Problems of Futures Research in the Social Sciences," *Futures* (September 1968), 1:1, 49.

82. Donella H. Meadows, Dennis L. Meadows, Jorgen Randers, and William W. Behrenes III, *The Limits to Growth* (New York: Universe Books, 1972).

83. Ibid., 142.

84. Science Policy Research Unit, University of Sussex, "The Limits to Growth Controversy," *Futures* (February 1973), 5:1. Special issue.

85. Christopher Freeman, "Malthus with a Computer," *Futures* (February 1973), 5:1, 7.

86. Ibid., 10.

87. Milos Zeman, "Futurology—Illusion or Reality? *Futures* (March 1971), 3:1, 10.

88. Freeman, "Malthus," 8.

89. Gordon, *Methods of Futures Research*, 25.

90. Moore, *Social Change*, 3.

91. Denis F. Johnston, "Forecasting Methods in the Social Sciences," in Japan Society of Futurology, comp., *Challenges from the Future*, 3 vols. (Tokyo: Kodansha, 1970), I, 138.

92. Bell, "Twelve Modes of Prediction," 869.

CHAPTER 3

Methods of social forecasting: projection based on psychological factors

INTRODUCTION

As J. Victor Baldridge divided social forecasting approaches into two kinds—a distinction comparable to the one between the previous and the present chapter—and assigned figureheads, he said, "Where Marx had focused upon the technological, economic, structural, and materialistic base as the prime agents of social change, Weber stressed the role of future orientations, ideological components, and value positions."[1] Max Weber, in what has come to be his best-known work, had declared the Protestant ethos to be a determinant in the rise of capitalism, and so lent credence to the notion that certain psychological factors can presage subsequent sociocultural realities.[2] He is the intellectual father of the methods described here, and indeed of the method which is to be proposed.

The title of grandfather belongs to the sagest observer of American life, Alexis de Tocqueville. In his introduction to *Democracy in America*, de Tocqueville said that the value of equality had long been governing societal transformations: "The noble has gone down the social ladder, and the commoner has gone up; the one descends as the other rises. Every half-century brings them nearer to each other, and they will soon meet."[3] The egalitarian impulse was strong enough to shape the future.

That attitudinal factors can prefigure social changes, rather than the other way around, is a concept which John McHale felt has been insufficiently considered in futures research,[4] but nonetheless it has not been ignored. Harold Lasswell, for example, urged that the social process be regarded as the attempt of men to optimize their values.[5] Wilbert Moore added his endorsement with the proposal that change is universally in the direction of what is idealized.[6] The attractiveness of this forecasting tactic was explained by Willis Harman:

> one argument for giving needs-values-beliefs a central place in the methodology is that they appear to be in some sense more fundamental than either events or trends in social descriptors. A second reason has to do with economy.[7]

That is, beyond pretensions to elemental truth, this approach has the advantages offered by parsimonious theory and method.

Work which has been done in this vein can be placed under four headings: images of the future, values, aspirations, and needs (or motives).

IMAGES OF THE FUTURE

In 1961 there appeared in English translation a book entitled *The Image of the Future*, written by a Dutch sociologist, which still continues to stimulate people concerned with the study of the future. In a sentence, its thesis was: "The future course of history is charted by the history of thought about this future."[8] Its author, Fred L. Polak, examined the long strains of utopian and eschatological thought in Western civilization and judged them to be premonitory. He determined to his satisfaction that what a people see as their future is what in fact their future will be. "Once the image of the future begins to decay and lose its vitality, however, the culture cannot long survive."[9] This is the melancholic state of affairs in contemporary life, he asserted,[10] although in the end he could not deny the possibility of redemption.[11]

An expansive work, it is open to a number of questions. The manner in which Polak determined a past culture's image of the future was not noticeably objective. Whatever the standards were which allowed for the selection of thinkers he discussed, they were unclear. There is no reason not to believe that he simply picked those who fit his scheme and ignored others. Moreover, Polak's prolix treatment aside, these historical images of the future hardly seem to have been successfully prophetic, since neither utopias nor eschatologies did materialize.

Similar questions can be raised about his analysis of the contemporary future. He stated that no vivid images of the future now exist, when they proliferate in the popular arts. In fact, he himself contributed to the stock of images of the future with the eschatology which he implied. Even if it were granted that present-day images of the future pale in comparison to previous ones, this could well be a comment on decreasing fearfulness about the future, rather than on the advent of inconceivable terrors.

In short, if one adopts Polak's idea, it must be done for reasons other than the science of his argument. Nevertheless, the concept has caught the fancy of many futurists. Typical of these is the French planner Pierre Bertaux, who referred to "the dynamic force of a strong and rich and powerful image of the future" which can draw a society on.[12] More impertinent was Elise Boulding, when she charged that the debility of modern-day images of the future extends into the field of futures research too.[13]

Most influential, perhaps, are Wendell Bell and James A. Mau, editors of *The Sociology of the Future,* a collection of articles much influenced by Polak. This indebtedness was acknowledged in their own piece before they derived their theory of social change:

> Motivated individuals, acting as individuals or members of groups, their images of the future, and their resultant behaviors are the key elements that keep the system moving and bring a future into being in the present. The behavior is viewed as largely the result of decisions (or in some cases decisions not to decide), which are essentially choices among alternative

futures. . . . Images of the future are of critical importance in influencing which of the alternative futures becomes present reality.[14]

Bell and Mau claimed that images of the future could be manipulated by concerned social scientists to bring about movement toward "the good."[15] But as was pointed out in a severe review of the book, "Whose good are we to covet? Nixon's, Brezhnev's, Mao's, the 'silent majority's,' the 'vocal minority's,' yours, or mine?"[16]

Bell and Mau's high hopes are an indication of the naivete which lingers about the image-of-the-future concept. Although the notion is initially appealing in its simplicity, there is no empirical evidence at all that it is also predictive. Images of the future may well belong to the class of articulations which occur on the surface of a culture in response to topical difficulties, but which reveal little of the more profound forces that direct it through time. (The images of science fiction, it can be gratuitously added, may also belong to this class.)

VALUES

By comparison, values would seem to be deeper-seated personality attributes and of potentially greater worth in prediction. Psychologists have long recognized the directive force that values exert upon individuals,[17] so no great conceptual leap was involved for futurists to theorize that they may also be a directive force for societies.

F. E. Emery, in an important article on social forecasting strategies, suggested "the direct study of what is valued," since changes in values—which he equated with ideals—precede changes in a society as it undergoes the never-ending process of adaptation.[18] To uncover the values of a people, he turned to C. West Churchman, who had proposed that

we can determine whether any specific individual or society is pursuing a certain ideal over a specified period of time. The criteria are as follows:

1.) The efficiency of the means chosen for any end approximating the ideal tends to increase over time.

2.) The probability of choosing these more efficient means increases over time.

3.) The desire (intention) for the ideal tends to increase over time.[19]

In a later work Churchman occasionally touched on the idea of values ("what the group really wants") as predictors, but was apparently willing to leave the empirical effort to others.[20]

The usefulness of values in social forecasting was considered at greater length by Robin Williams:

> Values have consequences. This statement would be made true only by definition if one said, "Values are criteria of desirability that affect selections among alternative modes of behavior." We intend this assertion, however, as an empirical claim: given the existence or nonexistence of a value standard as ascertained by specified observational operations at Time 1, we predict a different outcome at Time 2 under otherwise identical conditions, depending upon the presence or absence of the value in question.[21]

But how are the value standards to be ascertained? Williams had a procedural suggestion which will prove to be of importance to this study: "One obvious and accessible source of data for a national inventory of value patterns is the output of the mass media."[22]

The use of values, then, has been proposed several times over. Unfortunately, there has been little subsequent research. One reason for this—if not the major reason—is that the difficulties which ensue after accepting the idea and getting down to work are formidable. For all that people talk about values, there is little agreement on just what they are. The great explications of value systems have yet to be written.[23] Thus, for the futurist who is determined to use this strategy, an intellectual excursion would first be necessary which might well dwarf his forecasting venture.

As a result, the few attempts to predict from values have been insubstantial. Harman, for example, took stock of the conspicuous values of 1969 and opined:

In essence, what we proposed is that some aspects of the present situation may be interpreted as indications of a possible shift in the basic premises of the culture, somewhat as the historical process called the Protestant Reformation involved a shift of predominant beliefs from the theological view of the Middle Ages to the economic view of the modern world.[24]

From the perspective of several years later, it is less certain that such a change in the constitution of the culture has taken place. As Herman Kahn observed:

a great deal of impetus behind the prophecy that humanist left values will quickly spread throughout our society is based upon the hope for their diffusion held by people sympathetic to those values. We cannot live without dreams, but we should not permit our fantasies to substitute for the real and concrete future.[25]

If the study of values is to be of any utility in social forecasting, it must itself advance beyond the point of being value ridden.

ASPIRATIONS

Factors baser than values were what the social psychologist Hadley Cantril came upon in his search for the personality variables which underlie social change. These he called "aspirations." In Cantril's theory men ceaselessly aspire

to experience satisfactions that are permeated with value overtones. As human beings, we seem to seek a quality of experience far different from that sought by any other type of organism we know. Man's capacity to experience value satisfactions propels him to learn and to devise new ways of behaving that will enable him both to extend the range and heighten the quality of value satisfactions and to insure the repeatability of those value satisfactions already experienced.[26]

Of course, as there are some conditions men aspire to, there are others they shy away from. These hopes and fears together form the roadbed of social change. They direct the succession of social structures and political systems, which are to be regarded as "experiments," provisionally consolidating the gains made as aspirations are realized.[27] Since this striving of mankind, this need to garner value satisfactions, "will in the long run force any institutional framework to accommodate it,"[28] aspirations are the key to history.

And so, if aspirations could be tabulated, the social future would be more discernible. Cantril instituted a measuring instrument which he called the "Self-Anchoring Striving Scale" and administered it to a large sample population in thirteen countries the world around. A respondent would be asked to describe his wishes and hopes for "the best possible life," which then defined the top of the ten-step ladder scale; the bottom was "the worst possible life he could imagine."[29] Having these two extremes, he was then asked to indicate where he was now situated on the ladder, where he had stood five years before, and where he estimated he would be five years in the future. He was additionally asked for his aspirations and fears regarding his country.

The conclusion was that "all people without exception expected an improvement in the future both for themselves and for their country."[30] Improvement meant the amenities of industrialized civilization.

All the findings would indicate that the spirit of the century is one in which the standards of Western society would clearly prevail.

This is understandable enough. For the vast majority of people's hopes and fears were found to revolve around the complex of well-being rather simply defined in terms of a decent standard of living, a more secure family life with opportunities for children. In underdeveloped countries, an appreciable number of people hopes for technological advances which would speed improvements in their standard of living. Modern technology with all its faults obviously tends to alleviate the burdens people have borne for so many centuries and opens up more opportunities for more satisfactions in terms of greater security, better health, and self-development in a variety of ways.[31]

Americans were polled three times with the Self-Anchoring Striving Scale during the period ending with 1971, which allowed for some comparisons:

> The American people continue to be preoccupied with two matters—health and their standard of living. These two items were cited most frequently as both hopes and fears in 1959, 1964, and 1971, though they were mentioned with considerably less frequency in 1971.

> Although the chief hopes and fears expressed by Americans have changed little in the past twelve years, Americans appear to be less preoccupied with what has traditionally comprised the American Dream. This conclusion can be drawn from the decreased frequency with which people mentioned, as either hopes or fears, higher standard of living, fulfillment of aspirations for children, owning a home, availability of leisure time, and assurance of a happy old age.[32]

Over the twelve-year term Americans felt they had progressed in their personal lives nearly a full step on the ten-step ladder and were optimistic about continuing to gain.[33]

While Cantril's procedure provides much-needed data about some present-day concerns, it is wanting as a forecasting device. First, as he himself admitted, the full array of human aspirations are not tapped with the Self-Anchoring Striving Scale.[34] Respondents are unlikely to mention needs—sexual ones, for instance—which they think may cause them to lose face with the interviewer. Nor, needless to say, will subconscious aspirations be picked up.

Second, even if all aspirations were collected, it is not certain that this order of psychological factors can be finely predictive. Aspirations by definition are always optimistic, and although it may be true that in the long-term the course of mankind is ascending, in the short-term this is not the case by any means. Aspirations can not foretell downturns in the way that they presumably do advances.

NEEDS

"In trying to account for the genesis of aspirations, of what a person wants and longs for, one of course lands squarely in the area loosely called 'motivation'," Cantril had remarked, indicating that aspirations had their wellspring in motives or needs.[35] Values are also undergirded by needs. Everett Hagen wrote, "Needs are inner forces causing general tendencies. Values are the standards which determine the type of action by which (including the objects toward which) one will give vent to one's needs."[36] Being more primal than values or aspirations, needs are held to be largely beyond the conscious retrieval of the possessor.[37] Nonetheless, despite their obscurity, psychological researchers generally testify to the great influence of needs upon behavior.[38] Their understanding is that a human relentlessly tries, by one means or another, to satisfy deep-lying needs he is scarcely aware of. If a person's needs were somehow known in detail, then predictions about his future behavior could logically be made.

Similarly, large-scale social change might be anticipated by the needs of the members of a society. This was the position Hagen arrived at when he attempted to give reason to one aspect of social change, that of economic growth. Upon finding the standard theories inadequate, he turned to the idea of prevailing psychological attributes as the cause, specifically to a need for innovation instilled as a reaction to a loss of status by a previous generation.[39] For Hagen, "Culture is transmitted from generation to generation not primarily in memory but in personality."[40] In a footnote he gave one instance which was not of an economic nature to show how this theory might apply throughout the socio-cultural environment:

> For example, I suggest that millions of persons in the United States believed Senator Joseph McCarthy's statements in the early 1950's about the sinister network of Communists that threatened American life not because of any evidence they

read but because the concept of a mysterious force which threatened them matched and confirmed a sense of alarm they had felt in infancy and childhood at arbitrary threatening forces (perhaps authoritarian forces) in their lives, a sense which of course has been reinforced and deepened during the depression of the 1930's and World War II.[41]

Hagen's speculations on the importance of needs in historical change were based on the work of Henry A. Murray, who produced, said Hagen, "the classic discussion of needs."[42] In 1938 Murray published *Explorations in Personality*, which contained the results of a sustained team effort at the Harvard Psychological Clinic to sort out the components of personality, including the variety of needs. According to his definition, which has served much motivational research since then, needs are realized in transformations:

A need is a construct (a convenient fiction or hypothetical concept) which stands for a force (the physicochemical nature of which is unknown) in the brain region, a force which organizes perception, apperception, intellection, conation and action in such a way as to transform in a certain direction an existing, unsatisfying situation.[43]

Among those informed by Murray's investigation was another person interested in getting at the causes of economic development, the social psychologist David McClelland.[44] In contrast to Hagen, McClelland proceeded empirically; he wanted to thoroughly test the predictive ability of one particular need, the need for achievement. The significance of McClelland's study to the developing science of social forecasting stems from its carefulness as much as from its content.

As reported in the book *The Achieving Society*, McClelland and his associates first studied a number of preliterate cultures to see if there were any relationship at all between the level of need for achievement and economic activity.[45] To ascertain need for achievement levels, he examined the content of folk tales widespread in each tribe, feeling that the stories suited the people who treasured them and reflected motivational norms. These stories were rated for their achievement imagery by means of coding procedures which had been employed in the measurement of the motives of individual subjects taking projective tests, such as Murray's well-known Thematic Apperception Test. To determine the economic state of the cultures, McClelland computed from anthropological data the approximate percentage of full-time entrepreneurs. Based on the figures from forty-five tribes, the two factors—need for achievement levels and entrepreneurial activity—were found to be closely associated. Now the question became, does one of the two antecede the other?

The hypothesis, derived from Max Weber, was that a high need for achievement in a society came first and predicted subsequent economic growth. McClelland wanted to test this with modern societies, but they lacked the folk tales which he had previously used as a source of data. Was there anything comparable? He decided on children's readers, since they convey in imaginative form culturewide motivational lessons. Quoting Margaret Mead, he said, "A culture has to get its values across to its children in such simple terms that even a behavioral scientist can understand them."[46]

A sample of readers from 1925 for twenty-three countries was assembled, and twenty-one stories were selected at random for each.[47] Two trained judges scored the stories for their accounts of striving and achieving, and need for achievement ratings were assigned to the twenty-three countries.

The next problem was to compute economic growth.[48] After some deliberation McClelland fashioned an index which combined national income and electrical output figures. Regression equations were then established to predict economic gains to 1950. Plus or minus deviations from what was expected told of greater or lesser economic growth.

The data strongly confirmed the hypothesized relationship.[49] Levels of the need for achievement were positively correlated with subsequent economic development; the reverse relationship did not exist. Thus high need for achievement in a society was shown to forecast rapid economic growth.

CONCLUSION

A society's image of the future, or values, or aspirations, have been variously held to indicate its future. However, only for the motives of a people has this been shown to be the case. David McClelland, in a study marked by its discrimination and rigor, found that a high or low need for achievement in a society foretold greater or lesser economic advance.

Since McClelland's work continues to be well received,[50] it can be said that one personality element has been clearly demonstrated to be predictive of socio-cultural change. No wonder McClelland felt able to claim, "These results serve to direct our attention as social scientists away from an exclusive concern with the external events in history, to the 'internal' psychological concerns that in the long run determine what happens in history."[51]

McClelland's exploration into the factors of social change will serve as the basis of the proposed forecasting method.

NOTES

1. J. Victor Baldridge, "Images of the Future and Organizational Change: The Case of New York University," in Wendell Bell and James A. Mau, eds., *The Sociology of the Future* (New York: Russell Sage Foundation, 1971), 272.

2. Max Weber, *The Protestant Ethic and the Spirit of Capitalism*, trans. Talcott Parsons (New York: C. Scribner's, 1930).

3. Alexis de Tocqueville, *Democracy in America*, 2 vols., ed. Phillips Bradley (New York: Vintage Books, 1945), I, 6.

4. John McHale, "Problems in Social and Cultural Forecasting," in Japan Society of Futurology, comp. *Challenges from the Future*, 3 vols. (Tokyo: Kodansha, 1970), I, 10.

5. Harold D. Lasswell, "The Changing Image of Human Nature: The Socio-Cultural Aspect (Future-Oriented Man)," *American Journal of Psychoanalysis* (1966), 26:2, 162.

6. Wilbert E. Moore, *Social Change* (Englewood Cliffs, N.J.: Prentice-Hall 1963), 18.

7. Willis H. Harman, "Contemporary Social Forces and Alternative

Futures," *Journal of Research and Development in Education* (Summer 2:4, 69.

8. Fred L. Polak, *The Image of the Future*, 2 vols. (New York: Oceana Publications, 1961), I, 318.

9. Ibid., I, 49.

10. Ibid., II, 89.

11. Ibid., II, 357.

12. Pierre Bertaux, "The Future of Man," in William R. Ewald, Jr., ed., *Environment and Change: The Next Fifty Years* (Bloomington: Indiana University Press, 1968), 19.

13. Elise Boulding, "Futurology and the Imagining Capacity of the West," in Magoroh Maruyama, ed., *1970 American Anthropological Association Cultural Futurology Symposium: Pre-Conference Volume* (Minneapolis: University of Minnesota, 1970), 2:29.

14. Wendell Bell and James A. Mau, "Images of the Future: Theory and Research Strategies," in Bell and Mau, eds., 18.

15. Ibid., 35.

16. Toby E. Huff, "Articulating Images: The Sociology of Illusion," *Society* (May-June, 1973), 10:4, 80.

17. Edwin P. Hollander, *Principles and Methods of Social Psychology* (New York: Oxford University Press, 1971), 19.

18. F. E. Emery, "The Next Thirty Years: Concepts, Methods, and Anticipations," *Human Relations (August 1967), 20:3*, 207.

19. C. West Churchman and Russell L. Ackoff, The Democratization of Philosophy," *Science and Society* (Fall 1949), XIII:4, 335.

20. C. West Churchman, *Prediction and Optimal Decision, Philosophical Issues of a Science of Values* (Englewood Cliffs, N.J.: Prentice-Hall, 1961),358.

21. Robin M. Williams, Jr., "Individual and Group Values," in Bertram M. Gross, ed., *Social Intelligence for America's Future* (Boston: Allyn & Bacon, 1969), 169.

22. Ibid., 177.

23. Nicholas Rescher, "The Future as an Object of Research," in Kurt Baier and Nicholas Rescher, eds., *Values and the Future* (New York: The Free Press, 1969), 108.

24. Harman, "Alternative Futures," 83.

25. Herman Kahn and B. Bruce-Briggs, *Things to Come* (New York: The Macmillan Co., 1972), 246.

26. Hadley Cantril, *The Pattern of Human Concerns* (New Brunswick, N.J.: Rutgers University Press, 1965), 10.

27. Ibid., 19.

28. Ibid., 321.

29. Ibid., 22.

30. Ibid., 318.

31. Ibid., 313.

32. Albert H. Cantril and Charles W. Roll, Jr., *Hopes and Fears of the American People* (New York: Universe Books, 1971), 18.

33. Ibid., 20.

34. Hadley Cantril, *Human Concerns*, 26.

35. Ibid., 8.

36. Everett E. Hagen, *On the Theory of Social Change: How Economic Growth Begins* (Homewood, Ill.: Dorsey Press, 1962), 113.

37. A. H. Maslow, *Motivation and Personality* (New York: Harper & Row, 1954), 66.

38. Edward J. Murray, *Motivation and Emotion* (Englewood Cliffs, N.J.: Prentice-Hall, 1964), 7.

39. Hagen, *Theory of Social Change*, 200.

40. Ibid., 152.

41. Ibid.

42. Ibid., 100.

43. Henry A. Murry, *Explorations in Personality* (New York: John Wiley & Sons, 1938), 124.

44. Bernard Weiner, *Theories of Motivation: From Mechanism to Cognition* (Chicago: Markham Publishing Co., 1972), 173.

45. David C. McClelland, *The Achieving Society* (Princeton, N.J.: D. Van Nostrand Co., 1961), 63-70.

46. Ibid., 71.

47. Ibid., 71-75.

48. Ibid., 80-89.

49. Ibid., 93.

50. Ole R. Holsti, "Content Analysis," in Gardner Lindzey and Elliot Aronson, eds., *The Handbook of Social Psychology*, 2d ed., 5 vols. (Reading, Mass.: Addison-Wesley Publishing Co., 1968), II, 662.

51. McClelland, *Achieving Society*, 105.

CHAPTER 4

The proposed forecasting method and its data in brief

THE BASIS OF THE METHOD

In the attempt to develop a new social forecasting method, an inviting prospect is offered with the idea that attributes of the personalities of individual members presage the course of their collective culture. Simply by determining the kind and degree of these attributes, predictions of their society's future could be made. If this approach were sound, then it would be possible to skirt the task of comprehending in detail the near-impenetrable dynamics of large-scale social systems. Predictive efforts in sociology have been ensnared in that thicket, but here would be the promise of a means to cut through.

Of a number of psychological elements alleged to underlie social change, only needs, or motives, have passed close scrutiny.[1] It would seem reasonable to try to enlarge on David McClelland's gain by taking a fuller roster of needs into account, as well as a fuller portion of the sociocultural environment. If one need is predictive, perhaps others are; if economic growth can be forecasted, it is conceivable that more pervasive features of social change can be anticipated.

The central proposition would be that the fundamental longings of a people prefigure future ways of life and societal arrangements.

Or, better put, that changes in the array of mass needs are predictive of changes in the nature of a society. For it is change from one point in time to another which must serve as the measure; in this context absolute statements have little utility. There are no criteria, no measuring sticks, for saying that a society is definitely one thing or another. How much belligerence is enough to describe a nation as bellicose? At what point is a threshold passed for a society to be labeled tolerant? Instead, pictures of a culture and predictions of change must be relative. A society can legitimately be described only as comparatively such-and-so, not absolutely; this will be the mode of discussion throughout.

So, a component of the nonvolitional sector of the human enterprise, mass needs, is held to exert great pressure on the socio-cultural environment, constantly seeking accommodation. A people's needs vary in time—as McClelland demonstrated with the need for achievement[2]—for reasons which are admittedly not understood. But what can be ventured is that their fluctuations eventually manage to bring about change. The inertia of social systems means that there will be a time lag between changes at the level of mass needs and changes in the manifest culture. By knowing the mass needs of a people at a point in time, the direction of subsequent socio-cultural modulation can be expected.

The job at hand is to present the makings of a social forecasting method which derives from this estimation of the power of mass needs. The underpinnings of the proposed method will be detailed, its pretensions sketched, and a trial executed.

So that the following discussion may be read with a specific instance in mind, it is American culture on which the method will be tried. Can broad changes in American life be anticipated a decade ahead through the use of the method being proposed? It was decided to study motivational change in America from 1950 to 1960, so as to forecast socio-cultural change from 1960 to 1970. These decennial dates were selected because they afforded the opportunity of using census data in the process of testing the trial forecast. Should the method survive the test, it will then be used to forecast the future through 1980, on the basis of variation in needs from 1960 to 1970.

MASS COMMUNICATIONS

Society is impossible without communication, without information being transferred between discrete units so as to produce integration. In pre-industrial cultures communication is almost exclusively face-to-face, but in technologized societies much of the information exchange is accomplished through the mass media of communications—newspapers, magazines, radio, films, records, television, books, comics, and other varieties which carry messages created for large and distant audiences. Some have argued that these large-scale message systems have actually fashioned mass society;[3] it is enough to say that mass communication and modern society fit one another and occur together.

According to Harold Lasswell, mass communications function to provide surveillance of the environment, to permit correlation of the parts of the society in responding to the environment, and to allow for the transmission of a social heritage.[4] To these three the sociologist Charles Wright added a fourth—the supplying of entertainment.[5] Paul Lazarsfeld and Robert Merton saw this last as the "narcotizing dysfunction of the mass media," balanced by two other functions—the conferral of status and the affirmation of social norms.[6] All in all, they said, "the mass media of communication operate toward the maintenance of the going social and cultural structure rather than toward its change."[7]

The conservative nature of mass communication accounts for the observation of many social scientists that its effects are severely circumscribed. The most authoratative statement of this came from Joseph Klapper, who summarized a vast body of communications studies when saying:

1. Mass communication ordinarily does not serve as a necessary and sufficient cause of audience effects, but rather functions among and through a nexus of mediating factors and influences.

2. These mediating factors are such that they typically render mass communication a contributory agent, but not the sole cause, in a process of reinforcing the existing conditions.[8]

In short, mass communications work cautiously in the interests of a society's preservation. This was ingeniously demonstrated by Warren Breed, who looked at items which the media refused to carry.[9] In his judgment, there was a clear-cut tendency to suppress that material which might expose flaws in the working of institutions. There simply cannot be much about mass communication which is provocative, or it could not carry out its primary function of knitting a modern society together.

The point being made here is that systems of mass communication fit well the large social units they service. The networks cover the society, their content suits it. Therefore, no injustice would be done if, to get at the changing nature of a culture, its message system were tapped. In fact, Norbert Wiener, the originator of the field of cybernetics, stated that this would be the sole means of comprehending a society.[10] If it is not the only means, it is at least among the more reasonable. Given the significance and ubiquity of the mass media, Ithiel de Sola Pool had cause to say that "most social facts worth studying are embedded in a process of communication."[11]

In a number of technical senses, too, mass communications offer a superior source of data on social change. Some of them have been noted by Denis McQuail:

> Amongst the attractions of mass media content as study material for the social scientist are its ready accessibility and the feasibility of a near-objective and quantitative approach. It appears in standardized forms which are stable over relatively long periods; it is also more open to comparative analysis than most cultural institutions or forms, and its overt meaning can be more readily relied upon as material for analysis.[12]

The material is accessible because it can be, and is, readily stored. Storage means that data for past years may always be culled; the Americans of 1950 cannot be interviewed, their society cannot be probed, but their media messages can certainly be examined. It is the promise of historical comparisons which makes recorded communication so valuable.

Additionally, when a researcher is faced with a social entity as immense as a society, data from the media provide a necessary conciseness. Since there are few sources of mass communication, a certain succinctness obtains.

And finally, because the researcher and his raw material are withdrawn from on-going "live" social systems, the result is an unobtrusive measure. Such a measure avoids the distortions created by the influence, no matter how subtle, of a data-collector upon a source, as during an interview. This is an especially important consideration when it comes to ascertaining needs, which respondents tend to misrepresent.

For a clearer picture of the sources of data in this study, a model of the process of mass communication drawn up by Bruce Westley and Malcolm Maclean is helpful[13](see Figure 1). At the far left the elements of the environment are represented by X's; they are selectively perceived by a source of information, who in turn enlists communicators; the communicators, who have additional perceptions of the environment, construct and convey messages to an audience. Critical system-maintaining information flows back to the communicator from the audience (dotted line); feedback also goes from the audience to the source, and from the communicator to the source.

First, to uncover the sort and extent of the public's unsatisfied

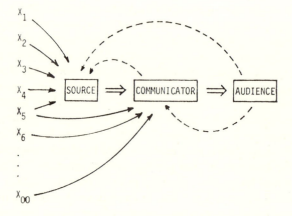

Fig. 1. The Westley-Maclean Model

needs, an order of messages from communicator to audience which are designed to invoke motives will be studied. The argument (as developed in the next chapter) will be that the communicators in this instance are so successful at recognizing the audience's needs and incorporating that knowledge into their messages, that all the researcher has to do is separate out the motivational appeals. The messages referred to are, needless to say, those of mass advertising.

It is felt that advertising is more telling about a people's needs than the children's readers which David McClelland used. The story books are likely to depict only acceptable motives, so some which are abroad in the culture but unappreciated would be strained out. Advertising is less constrained.

Put in terms of the Westley-Maclean model, the process of advertising is this: from an advertiser (the source) comes the impetus for a message which the staff of an advertising agency (the communicator) skilfully weds to a motivational appeal (whose genesis is in the return flow of information from audience to communicator) and then sends out through channels of communication.

The worth of this data source is contingent upon the existence of feedback in mass communications. While this point will be examined in greater detail in the following chapter, it is important here to reassert how conservative mass communication is, and how much it is in conformity with its audience—a fact which would be unlikely to occur unless there were a feedback provision included in the system. Several studies have revealed that the fiction published in popular novels and mass circulation periodicals mirrors the predominating values and norms of the culture.[14] In an interesting variation on this line of research, Russell Middleton showed that changes in family size depicted in mass magazine stories over forty years paralleled changes in actual fertility rates.[15] As Herbert Gans stated when investigating the role of the audience in movie-making, "One of the elements in the process by which movies (as well as other mass-media products) are created is that feedback takes place between the audience of that product and its creators."[16] There is a fundamental reciprocity involved in mass communication, a two-way flow of information,[17] and its existence explains why the communicator's message can be studied to learn about the audience's state of mind.

Referring again to the Westley-Maclean model, the second sort of information required is on the changing nature of the socio-cultural environment, symbolized by the X's. Since it is a function of the news to survey this environment and report on transformations,[18] data will be teased from this source.

Although the point will be raised again later, it should be explained early on that there is no faith here that the surveillance of social change by news-gathering institutions is thoroughly or accurately done. Instead, the idea is that changing proportions of certain categories of news stories reflect correspondingly proportional changes in the realities of the culture. The sorts of bias on the part of news-gatherers are assumed not to vary enough over a decade to corrupt this proportional data.

When the method is tested, there are to be five points of data collection. Mass needs will be uncovered through an analysis of mass advertising in the years 1950, 1960, and 1970; socio-cultural change will be appraised by means of an analysis of the news in 1960 and 1970. The change in the substratum of needs from 1950 to 1960 should be predictive of change in the manifest socio-cultural environment from 1960 to 1970. (Other data on the actualities of American life, as from the 1970 census, will also be cited to check the test forecast.) If the forecast of 1970 can be demonstrated to be accurate, then the change in the motives of Americans from 1960 to 1970 should have much to say about 1980.

CONTENT ANALYSIS

The procedures for extracting data from advertising and news belong to a group of techniques known collectively as content analysis. The most popular definition of content analysis was provided some years ago by Bernard Berelson: "Content analysis is a research technique for the objective, systematic and quantitative description of the manifest content of communications."[19] Lately, however, this definition has been supplanted by another from Ole Holsti: "Content analysis is any technique for making inferences by objectively and systematically identifying specified characteristics of messages."[20] What Holsti's definition adds is a "reason-why:" to draw inferences about such elements of the communications process as the stimuli, the communicator, the audience, the setting.

Holsti's definition is coming into fashion because it suits changes going on in the application of these techniques and the ambitions of analysts.[21] In the past content analysis was employed with exceeding prudence; Thomas Carney called this older variety "classical content analysis," in which word counts led little further than to the description of express content.[22] In contrast, he stated, stands "theoretically-oriented content analysis," the newer sort, where the recording of themes supports meaningful inferences.

> In these two cases, in every respect the classical content analysis is more objective than the theoretically-oriented one. Consequently, its overall immediate validity is incomparably greater. *But this does not make it the better content analysis.* A good content analysis is one that is as objective as the constraints of question and text upon it allow it to be. It is the *question* that counts, not the count itself.[23]

Given the sorts of queries it pursues, the present study would seem to belong to the "theoretically-oriented" category. Like other studies of this sort, as Carney implied, it is going to be troubled with the vexing problem of validity. The case that the data from mass advertising are a valid measure of mass needs must be closely examined.

NOTES

1. David C. McClelland, *The Achieving Society* (Princeton, N.J.: D. Van Nostrand Co., 1961).

2. Ibid., 99.

3. Marshall McLuhan, *Understanding Media: The Extensions of Man* (New York: New American Library, 1964), 19.

4. Harold D. Lasswell, "The Structure and Function of Communication," in Lyman Bryson, ed., *The Communication of Ideas* (New York: Harper & Row, 1948), 51.

5. Charles R. Wright, *Mass Communication: A Sociological Perspective* (New York: Random House, 1959), 16.

6. Paul F. Lazarsfeld and Robert K. Merton, "Mass Communication, Popular Taste, and Organized Social Action," in Bernard Rosenberg and David Manning White, eds., *Mass Culture* (Glencoe, Ill.: The Free Press, 1957), 464.

7. Ibid., 473.

8. Joseph T. Klapper, *The Effects of Mass Communication* (New York: The Free Press, 1960), 8.

9. Warren Breed, "Mass Communication and Socio-Cultural Integration," *Social Forces* (December 1958), 37:2, 114.

10. Norbert Wiener, *The Human Use of Human Beings, Cybernetics and Society* (New York: Avon Books, 1967), 25.

11. Ithiel de Sola Pool, "Symbols, Meaning and Social Sciences," in Lyman Bryson, ed., *Symbols and Values: An Initial Study* (New York: Cooper Square Publishers, 1964), 352.

12. Denis McQuail, *Toward a Sociology of Mass Communication* (London: Collier-Macmillan, 1969), 68.

13. Bruce H. Westley and Malcolm Maclean, "A Conceptual Model for Communications Research," *Journalism Quarterly* (Winter 1957), 35.

14. For one see Patricke Johns-Heine and Hans H. Gerth, "Value in Mass Periodical Fiction, 1921-1940," in Rosenberg and White, eds., *Mass Culture,* 226-34.

15. Russell Middleton, "Fertility Values in American Magazine Fiction, 1916-1956," *Public Opinion Quarterly* (Spring 1960), 24:1, 142.

16. Herbert J. Gans, "The Creator-Audience in the Mass Media: An Analysis of Movie Making," in Rosenberg and White, eds., *Mass Culture,* 315.

17. DeFleur, *Theories of Mass Communication* (New York: McKay, 1966), 94.

18. Wright, *Mass Communication,* 16.

19. Bernard Berelson, *Content Analysis in Communication Research* (Glencoe, Ill.: The Free Press, 1952), 18.

20. Ole R. Holsti, *Content Analysis for the Social Sciences and Humanities* (Reading, Mass.: Addison-Wesley Publishing Co., 1969), 14.

21. Thomas F. Carney, *Content Analysis* (Winnipeg: University of Manitoba Press, 1972), 5.

22. Ibid., 41.

23. Ibid., 48.

CHAPTER 5

Mass advertising as a source of data on mass needs

THE COMMUNICATIONS SYSTEM OF MASS ADVERTISING

Advertising, according to Daniel Starch, who spent a lifetime testing its effects, is "communication. It is the paid form of mass communication designed to influence people to favor a product in order to induce them to buy it. In other words, advertising is mass selling.[1] This definition will serve well. Perhaps it could be improved upon by enlarging the word "product" to "product, service, or idea," but the elliptical term will do for this study as it did for Starch. The definition ignores point-of-purchase advertising, or trade advertising or advertising to professionals, or any variety besides that intended for a mass audience and carried by mass media. It offers most where it stresses advertising as communication.

"A company can no more stay in business without advertising today than an individual can exist without communication with others," observed Leo Bogart, indicating the significance of this communications activity.[2] If advertising is effective, the advertiser thrives; if it is not effective, the advertiser succumbs. The importance, the urgency, of this order of communication for the advertiser cannot be overestimated.

The goal of advertising messages is nothing less than to change human behavior, specifically, to increase the public's consumption of the advertiser's wares. The advertiser would like this to happen abruptly, with sales zooming upwards, but if it takes place, it is usually incrementally, as Starch implied. As one of Martin Mayer's respondents said, "What advertising does is to move you closer' to buying the product."[3]

The advertising process consists of not only the purposeful messages from communicator to audience, but also includes, as do all communications systems which endure, a reverse flow of information back to the communicator from the audience.[4] This second aspect of the advertising process is the more ill-defined, certainly, but it is not feeble. By virtue of this feedback the messages of advertisers can stay on target. The Hartleys are among those to insist on the recognition of this fundamental feature of mass communication systems like advertising:

> Communication is interaction. It is usually a two-way process, involving stimulation and response among organisms, and it is both reciprocal and alternating. The response evoked by one communique in turn becomes a stimulus and a communique in its own right. In this way, in a series of communications, each may be both response and stimulus.

> This statement holds true even for mass communication situations, where the audience is not present to answer back. If the communication is at all successful, the audience responds in some way, and its response affects future communications. The length of time between the inception of a communique and the response does not alter the fact that the latter takes place and that it has an effect on the communicator. An advertiser, for example, may have to wait before the response of his audience to an advertisement becomes evident, but once it does, it then affects the course of future advertisements.[5]

For present purposes, then, there are four components to the communications system of advertising: (1) the mass audience; (2) the communicators, who are advertising agency personnel; (3) the messages in the form of advertisements; and (4) the stabilizing provision of feedback.

THE AUDIENCE OF MASS ADVERTISING

The desired audience of mass advertising contains all the members of a society able to effect purchases. Excluded are those few who are not potential consumers—the very young, the extremely indigent, the institutionalized. The audience, then, is nearly identical with the vital human stock of the society.

At the most elemental level, the members of the audience are characterized by their needs, by those "elements in an individual's personality, forever demanding to be satisfied, or more precisely, quieted for a brief interval by one experience of satisfaction, then arising to demand satisfaction again."[6] Without needs human beings would atrophy, claimed Ernest Dichter: "If a man or woman is completely satisfied, he or she will not seek to acquire anything more. In fact, without tension, without the arousal of an unfulfilled need, human beings, living things in general, would not act, do, think, behave at all."[7]

Needs energize people and function as "the most compelling inner determinants of behavior."[8] For Abraham Maslow, "The organism is dominated and its behavior organized by unsatisfied needs."[9] Therefore, an attempt to alter behavior, to spur consumption, would not be likely to succeed if it did not pertain to these longings.

But for all their insistence, needs are not readily contacted. They are held to exist far below the surface of behavior, beyond the awareness of their possessor, at best merely inferred by an observer.[10] Dealing with needs means "dealing with something subtle, complex, and shifting—with the devious aspirations of the human spirit," noted Walter Taplin in the course of his insightful reflections on the nature of advertising.[11] "Shifting" is a key word, for the needs of individuals and audiences do not remain constant; David McClelland's research revealed that nations' need for achievement levels varied substantially over time.[12] Because the needs of a people change, they are doubly difficult to reach.

Not only do an audience's needs present a nebulous and moving target for advertisers, but the audience's attention is hard to catch. Although the American people have been shown by poll to be quite favorably disposed to advertising,[13] the competition for their eye is so intense that people must use filtering mechanisms, if as Raymond Bauer and Stephen Greyser said in their authoritative study, "they are to survive amidst their complex world of stimuli."[14] Bauer and Greyser reported that the average family had 1,500 opportunities for exposure to advertisements every day;[15] that of these the average American adult is aware of only 76 advertisements, as measured by a hand counter;[16] and that of the 76 only 12 a day typically produced a reaction—9 positively and 3 negatively.[17]

These two points deserve to be made again, this time with reference to the question of how docile the audience for mass advertising is. First, interest is not captured without great difficulty: "The consumer is no helpless passive target of communications. He is an active defender of his time, energy, attention, and interests. The communication process is one in which the audience plays a deliberate role in selecting that to which it will attend."[18] And second, the audience's needs are not easily engaged:

> In fact the quickest way to dispose of the idea that the consumer is helpless before the dominant power of the advertiser is to examine the actual practice of the advertisers themselves . . . advertisers and their agents do in fact spend a great deal of time and money trying to discover who the potential consumers are and what they want. These are the rock-bottom questions which must be answered unless the risk and expense of any advertising campaign are to be enormously and quite unnecessarily increased. If the advertiser does not succeed in finding out what the consumer wants he is liable to lose a lot of money.[19]

In the process of mass advertising, it appears, the audience's state of mind is more the determinant than the determined.

But this flies in the face of the belief that a tractable audience's needs are actually created by advertising. A leading spokesman for this view is John Kenneth Galbraith, who maintained that advertising functions "to create desires—to bring into being wants that previously did not exist."[20] A thoughtful response to this charge came from George Katona:

> Consumption can be and has been stimulated by salesmanship, marketing, and advertising. But the extent of such influence is far too small to justify the broad statements that are made about advertising's creating our wants. Production and advertising, when in line with prevailing sociopsychological tendencies, do contribute to the actualization of the manifold wants that stimulate our mass consumption society.[21]

It is the "prevailing sociopsychological tendencies" which are in charge.

Galbraith's position may possibly hinge on a matter of definition. There are orders of wants; a want for a dishwasher is not the same as a want to escape from the demands and drudgery of the housewife's role (which later in this study will be categorized as a "need for autonomy"). The former refers to the mode of satisfaction, the latter to the original unsatisfied deep-lying need. If Galbraith meant that advertising creates demand for specific palliatives for basic needs, he was probably correct; if he meant that advertising creates the needs themselves, he was ceding to advertisers a power they may covet but demonstrably do not have and robbing the audience of what Bauer called their "obstinacy."[22]

But terminology aside, Galbraith would seem to assume a communications system devoid of mutuality, in which information traveled just one way, from a towering advertising industry to a submissive audience. This is a misconstruction of the dynamic process of mass communication in that it ignores the existence of feedback. Galbraith apparently subscribes to the first, the less informed, of the two models of communication which Bauer has sketched:

> First, the social model of communication: the model held by the general public, and by social scientists when they talk

about advertising, and somebody else's propaganda, is one of the exploitation of man by man. It is a model of one-way influence: the communicator *does* something to the audience, while to the communicator is generally attributed considerable latitude and power to do what he pleases to the audience. This model is reflected—at its worst—in such popular phrases as "brainwashing," "hidden persuasion," and "subliminal advertising."

The second stereotype—the model which *ought* to be inferred from the data of research—is of communication as a transactional process in which two parties each expect to give and take from the deal approximately equitable values.[23]

The second model would describe the process by which the audience manages to inform the advertisers about its needs and is in turn informed about what is being offered in the marketplace to placate those needs.

THE COMMUNICATORS IN MASS ADVERTISING

The urge to buy stems from unsatisfied wants or needs. The satisfaction of wants or needs is accomplished through the benefits derived from the purchase of goods or services or from the use of the goods or services purchased. Unless the consumer is convinced that these benefits will be forthcoming from the purchase and use of a particular product, he will not buy.

The problem the advertiser has, then, is to determine the wants or needs of the consumers in his market.[24]

So the advertisers and their advertising agencies, at their end of the communications channel, are much more resolute than the audience at its. They must find out, as surely as possible, the motives of the audience in order to compose appeals which will engage them. Edgar Crane expressed this imperative vividly:

Day after day, workers in the advertising agency toil at their desks. Night after night, lonely lights burn late in its offices.

Interoffice memos flit back and forth like bats at dusk. Cigarette stubs pile up on conference table ashtrays. Media buyers juggle rates and circulations. Researchers punch away at their calculating machines. Product and prospect are poked and prodded for inspiration. Finally, a copywriter puts words on paper.

The campaign theme may be brilliant and the copywriter may have chosen symbols and combined them into messages with great skill, but all his work and all the work of the advertising agency will sink without a trace unless someone had determined what motivates the prospect to act.[25]

Feedback from current campaigns can be a prime source of information on the state of consumers' needs. Effective advertising would indicate the motivational appeals which had struck a vein worth further mining; ineffective advertising would tell which appeals were fruitless. The problem with this is that it is difficult to discover whether a campaign is working.

Logically, increased sales of the advertised product should be the gauge of success, but while this may be the ultimate check, it does not suffice in the normal course of events.[26] In part this is due to the fitfulness of an extensive distribution system, which confounds the measurement of sales:

Ordinarily, a manufacturer's sales records do not reveal week-to-week or even month-to-month retail sales in individual markets. His records indicate shipments to distributors, but do not show the extent to which inventories at the wholesale or retail level are being built up or depleted over short periods of time.[27]

Even when sales can be accurately tallied, they "are influenced by the whole past history of its [the product's] advertising and of competitive advertising, rather than by just the campaigns of the moment."[28] Past advertising is just one of a number of extraneous factors which effect present sales; Neil Borden observed in the summary of his research on the economic effects of advertising that fundamental social and economic currents were much more significant in determining consumer demand than advertising could ever be.[29] In a sinking market, therefore, advertising which was effective might not be advertising that increased sales. "A case in point is the Bert and Harry Piel campaign which slightly (*very* slightly) increased the sale of Piels in the New York Metropolitan Area at a time when total beer sales were slipping fairly rapidly."[30]

Advertisers have therefore been forced to turn away from sales figures and to devise procedures for directly measuring communication performance. Among the better known of these is a test developed by Daniel Starch which has had great currency in the advertising industry. A sample of the people exposed to an advertisement is asked by interviewers from the Starch organization how much they recognize upon seeing it a second time. Three grades of response are established: the percentage of the audience that originally noted the advertisement; the percentage that had seen the name of the advertiser; and the percentage that had read more than half the copy.[31] Another test of the same sort, but somewhat more rigorous, was developed by Gallup and Robinson, Inc. In this recall procedure, less prompting is done by the interviewer than during the Starch recognition method. "It is clear that this method puts a heavy burden upon the reader's memory and that the remembered impressions of content are substantial evidence of effective communication of advertising messages."[32]

Other methods try to get at attitude changes resulting from advertising. For example, the Schwerin Research Corporation initiated a procedure by which an audience in a theater is shown a number of advertisements and then tested for brand preference changes.[33] The relative success of different appeals is also measured by eliciting inquiries. In one version of this approach, known as split-run testing, two different advertisements for the same product can be compared when they are printed in alternate copies of the same issue of a publication. The one which brings in the most inquiries (or perhaps coupon returns) is judged the better.[34]

All in all, the battery of testing methods ensures some degree of feedback and some evidence of how successful various appeals are. But this is not the sum of the information flowing from audience to advertiser. More knowledge is solicited, since there is always the hope of finding out more about the dimensions of exploitable needs. Besides, as Sandage and Fryburger said, "motivation patterns change,"[35] and advertisers must keep on their trail. The result is that the advertising industry has mounted a considerable effort at scouting out needs.

Motivation research, as carried out for advertisers by psychologists like Ernest Dichter (whom Vance Packard referred to warningly as "the most famed of these depth probers"),[36] is usually accomplished in face-to-face interviews by means of such exercises as word associations, sentence completions, cartoon fill-ins, and Thematic Apperception Tests.[37] These methods are thought to bypass respondents' defenses and plumb needs which are likely to be "vague, inaccessible, or ego-threatening."[38] Since this sort of investigation may constitute a violation of privacy, motivation research has remained controversial. Packard reported with distress:

> People's subsurface desires, needs, and drives were probed in order to find their points of vulnerability. Among the subsurface motivating factors found in the emotional profile of most of us, for example, were the drive to conformity, need for oral stimulation, yearning for security. Once these points of vulnerability were isolated, the psychological hooks were fashioned and baited and placed deep in the merchandising sea for unwary prospective customers.[39]

This may be an accurate picture of the design, but the actualities have been less alarming. The record of motivation research over the years has been uneven, and to some extent it has gone out of fashion.[40] Nevertheless, it remains a useful instrument.

In the end, though, the greatest volume of information on needs still comes informally. John David Lewis found evidence to suggest that the demand for communication from the mass audience back to the communicators may be satisfied by feedback among the personnel of the communicators' own organization.[41] This may be one part of it; another is the product of nothing more than the intuitions of advertising men as they put their minds to the problem of making contact at basic levels with vast numbers of people. Exactly how their instincts are formed remains a mystery, although it is clear that some have better intuitions than others, and that the more adept come to have more influence in the process of constructing advertisements. It is due to their perceptiveness that the needs of the audience get communicated and incorporated into successful advertising messages.[42]

"The continuous pressure is to create ads more and more in the image of audience motives and desires."[43] To a great extent the ability of the advertising industry to do this, and to keep at the heels of the elusive needs of the public, is a function of the immensity of the effort. Taplin, recognizing this, wrote, "What we are confronted with in advertising is one of the most massive possible attempts to influence the conduct of human beings—an attempt which by its sheer weight and long continuance could hardly have failed, if only by accident, to get well below the surface of behavior."[44] The attempt is indeed massive, for American business annually invests $20 billion in it.[45] The amount of human exertion results, according to Mayer, in advertising men dying on the average ten years sooner than other American males.[46] The degree of financial and human commitment to the institution of advertising in recent decades has caused it to loom larger and larger on the American landscape.

Among those who have been struck with the prowess of the advertising industry is Marshall McLuhan:

Any expensive ad represents the toil, attention, testing, wit, art, and skill of many people. Far more thought and care go into the composition of any prominent ad in a newspaper or magazine than go into the writing of their features and editorials. Any expensive ad is as carefully built on tested foundations of public stereotypes of "sets" of established attitudes, as any skyscraper is built on bedrock. Since highly skilled and perceptive teams of talent cooperate in the making of an ad for any established line of goods whatever, it is obvious that any acceptable ad is a vigorous dramatization of communal experience. No groups of sociologists can approximate the ad teams in the gathering and processing of exploitable social data. The ad teams have billions to spend annually on research and

testing of reactions, and their products are magnificent accumulations of material about the shared experience and feeling
of the entire community.[47]

These "magnificent accumulations of material," the advertisements,
clearly merit study, then.

THE ADVERTISEMENT

An awareness of the needs of the audience is put to work in the
creation of advertisements. These carefully contrived messages are
designed to invoke the public's needs and to promote purchasable
gratification. "Advertising thus performs the function of interpreting
the want-satisfying qualities of services, products, or ideas in terms
of the needs and desires of consumers."[48]

At least, this dual nature—in having reference both to the advertiser's product and to the audience's needs—describes the sort of
advertisements which are germane to the present study. There is a
second type of advertisement, less ambitious, in which the product
is featured to the exclusion of any further appeal, as a tire advertisement that contains only the price and specifications of the tire.
Borden called these "direct-action advertisements," since their intention is so forthright, and contrasted them to the more circuitous
"indirect-action advertisements," whose objective is "to build the
reputations of the brands advertised and to enhance the wantability
of the branded products offered through building mental associations relating to them."[49]

Rather than use Borden's "direct-action" and "indirect-action"
labels, which pertain to the intent of an advertisement (something
not always easy to agree on), the terms "nonassociative" and "associative" will be employed here. They represent little gain in elegance, but have the advantages offered by objective criteria. In a
nonassociative advertisement, all the ingredients refer to what is
being sold; in an associative advertisement, the product is linked
with something extrinsic to it, which the advertiser has gone afield
to find. Such an advertisement "hopes to set off the product as something pretty wonderful by draping around it as many activating and

Would you let her freeze in the winter?

Of course not!

And right now is the best time to replace your old air conditioner with York.

Your York Dealer has an early-season offer.

No down-payment, up to five years to pay; you pay nothing 'til spring.

If you're spending money on your air conditioning system, now is the time to replace it—with an advanced York

unit that cools quietly.

York's Champion II whole-house comfort system is dependable. Trouble-free. And it's a beauty!

Only 18 inches high.

Stop spending money on service, parts and repairs—and start living comfortably.

Mail the coupon now for complete facts on York's advanced air conditioner, and details on your York Dealer's convenient payment plan for homeowners.

York Information Center
P.O. Box 8646 • Phila., Pa. 19101

YORK
DIVISION OF BORG-WARNER CORPORATION

☐ Have York Dealer phone and arrange for free air conditioning estimate
☐ Send me more information and name of nearby York Authorized Dealer

Name _____

Address _____

City _____ State _____ Zip _____

Telephone Number _____ Res. _____ 37

York. The air conditioning people.

We heat-cool: Homes, Buildings, Ships, Cars. Everything. We make plant refrigeration systems, Icemakers.

It is the need-for-dominance which this advertisement is addressed to; that is, the need to control the physical and social environment. (From January 30, 1970 issue of *Life*. Reproduced with permission of York.)

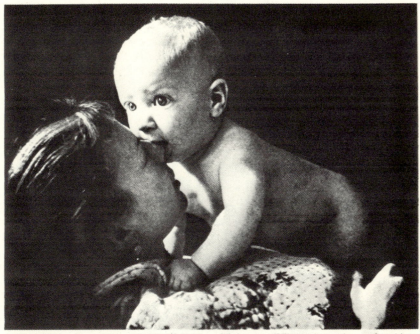

A LITTLE NIPPER brings big responsibilities . . . MONY's 'ADD-ON' life insurance helps you meet them. A basic MONY policy can help you take care of your present needs. (If the face amount is $5,000 or more, it even entitles you to a discount.) As your family responsibilities grow, you can help meet them by adding on low-cost MONY *riders.*

MONY'S 'ADD-ON' LIFE INSURANCE CAN GROW WITH YOUR FAMILY...AND SAVE YOU MONEY, TOO

'ADD-ON' was designed for the growing family. You buy an inexpensive MONY policy to cover basic needs. As your needs change, you adjust your policy by adding on low-cost MONY *riders* (subject, of course, to MONY's reasonable underwriting requirements). It's the easier, *thrifty* way! MONY's booklet tells you more about it. Get *your* copy.

CHILDREN'S EDUCATION. With MONY's inexpensive 'ADD-ON' riders, you can be certain there would be money to help send your youngsters to college if you were not around.

LIFETIME RETIREMENT INCOME. With 'ADD-ON' you can help provide for your own future, too . . . assure yourself of a steady retirement income that you cannot outlive.

Before you buy any life insurance, find out more about MONY's 'ADD-ON'. Send for free booklet today. Learn how you can get life insurance that is right for you, and save money, too.

MONY, Dept. L460, Broadway at 55th St., New York 19, New York

Please send me a copy of MONY's free booklet on 'ADD-ON'.

Name_____

Address_____

City_____County_____Zone__State_____

Occupation_____Birth Date_____

MUTUAL OF NEW YORK

The Mutual Life Insurance Company Of New York, New York, N. Y.
Sales and service offices located throughout the United States and in Canada

For Life, Accident & Sickness, Group Insurance, Pension Plans, **MONY TODAY MEANS MONEY TOMORROW!**

The cuteness of the baby would appeal the readers' need-for-nurturance, both coders judged. (From April 25, 1960 issue of *Life*. Reproduced with permission of the Mutual Life Insurance Company of New York.)

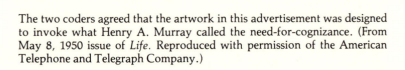

The two coders agreed that the artwork in this advertisement was designed to invoke what Henry A. Murray called the need-for-cognizance. (From May 8, 1950 issue of *Life*. Reproduced with permission of the American Telephone and Telegraph Company.)

pleasant associations as possible, by attaching to it all sorts of meanings with powerful motivational value in addition to its bare functional-use meanings."[50]

In the construction of an associative advertisement, how exactly is the motivational appeal put? Pierre Martineau gave a clue:

> Successful persuasion through advertising consists of far more than doing clever tricks with words. The consumer has developed a protective husk against mere word claims. . . . But other kinds of symbols, such as those in illustration, communicate images so much faster, with far less resistance, with much greater persuasiveness. The visual symbols are not just a support for word claims. They can contribute meanings and associations entirely apart and of much greater significance.[51]

The associations which are chosen to engage needs usually appear in the artwork of an advertisement. This is by no means always the case, but it is a convenient rule of thumb. Primary communication— at the level of needs—is achieved by illustrations, while words provide the follow-up, describing the qualities of what is being advertised. "Since the advent of pictures, the job of ad copy is as incidental and latent as the 'meaning' of a poem is to a poem, or the words of a song are to a song," said McLuhan, with only slight exaggeration.[52]

With an associative advertisement, then, it should be possible to separate the appeal to the audience's needs from the information regarding the product. This can be done by subtracting, through an act of the imagination, all product-related material from the advertisement; what remains should comprise the attempt to invoke needs. If, for instance, a transmission repair service were linked to Zsa Zsa Gabor, as occurred in a recent advertisement, then it would be exclusively Miss Gabor who received the investigator's attention.

In the present study this procedure shall be put to use on printed advertisements, since they are more accessible and lend themselves to closer scrutiny than advertising carried by the electronic media. Another reason for not using television commercials is that this mode was not well refined in 1950, the earliest date for which data is to be collected. However, in conception the method is applicable to all varieties of mass advertising.

CONCLUSION

> Human beings live in the realm of reality only very partially; they live much more in a realm of desires and illusions, and these determine their behaviour much more than any logical balance sheet or reasoning. The 'market of the individual' starts with whimsy and appeal, with the well-lit shop-window across the street. These are the elements which, in the end, really determine our behaviour. Myths, visions of happiness, and images in films, are basic elements in the consumer's behaviour. In the end, therefore, marketing is entirely determined by "mythical" and sometimes mystical phenomena. Here then, in order to be realistic and operational, it is necessary to discuss myths and the fabrication of the image, the whim and the irrational. To be rational about the future, we must discuss the irrational, because the beings who orient the future are themselves irrational.[53]

To determine what these alluring mythical images are which precede social change, Abraham Moles suggested examining "a number of handbills advertising a wide variety of things."[54] John McHale had the same idea when he proposed investigating "the ways in which viable images of future life styles and social forms are previsioned in the arts and communication media,"[55] specifically "novels, films, television, 'art,' comics, and advertisements."[56]

But the argument which has been made here is somewhat different. The express images contained in advertisements are not held to be predictive in and of themselves. At best, they reflect attitudes of the moment. Even images in the mass media which strive to be prophetic rarely are.[57]

Rather, the proposition here is that, in a certain order of mass advertising, the product to be sold is associated with images designed to invoke unfulfilled needs of the audience. These needs, which Taplin described as "numerous, complex, imperfectly known, and frequently changing,"[58] are sought out by the advertising industry with a resolve not found elsewhere. To learn what the advertising industry evinces it knows, a decoding of the motivational appeals made in mass advertising will be undertaken. This should produce data which could be taken as a measure of the needs extant in America at a given point in time. (With such a motivational profile in hand, and guided by McClelland's demonstration of the predictive nature of needs, forecasts can then be constructed.)

This approach owes much to the thinking of Marshall McLuhan, who maintained that advertisements

> express for the collective society that which dreams and uncensored behavior do in individuals. They give spatial form to hidden impulse and, when analyzed, make possible bringing into reasonable order a great deal that could not otherwise be observed or discussed. Gouging away at the surface of public sales resistance, the ad men are constantly breaking through into the *Alice in Wonderland* territory behind the looking glass which is the world of subrational impulses and appetites. Moreover, the ad agencies are so set on the business of administering major wallops to the buyer's unconscious, and have their attention so cencentrated on the sensational effect of their activities, that they unconsciously reveal the primary motivations of large areas of our contemporary existence.[59]

The acceptance of the McLuhanesque notion that advertising exposes the states-of-mind of its audience is not unique to this study. Sanford Dornbusch and Lauren Hickman supposed just this in their attempt to test David Riesman's theory of increasing other-directedness, saying," A basic assumption of this research is the belief that a shift in the verbal themes of consumer-goods advertising is likely to reflect a corresponding change in the values of the audience for that advertising."[60] They analyzed the content of the advertising in the *Ladies' Home Journal* from 1890 to 1956, looking for the proportion of advertisements that contained appeals to other-directedness. (Their findings, incidentally, were that the proportion did increase after the mid-point of 1921, as Riesman would have predicted, but that it dropped steeply from 1940 on, contrary to expectations.)

Dornbusch and Hickman's assumption of the reflective nature of mass advertising was preserved in Patricia Roe Morton's subsequent elaboration.[61] Besides the *Ladies' Home Journal,* she also used *McCall's* and *Good Housekeeping;* more indices of other-directedness were employed; and, the illustrations as well as the copy were subject to coding. (The results of the content analysis duplicated the earlier study's finding that other-directedness is on the decline in the United States.)

These studies are among the very few in which techniques of content analysis have been applied to mass advertising.[62] They are rarer still for assuming that their data can be a commentary on the audience, although analysts have been assured by Charles Osgood that inferences may be drawn from messages about the receivers as well as the producers.[63] And Morton's coding of advertising art work may be a methodological first.

Precedents set by those two studies will be followed here.

NOTES

1. Daniel Starch, *Measuring Advertising Readership and Results* (New York: McGraw-Hill, 1966), 2.

2. Leo Bogart, *Strategy in Advertising* (New York: Harcourt, Brace & World, 1967), 321.

3. Martin Mayer, *Madison Avenue, U.S.A.* (New York: Harper & Bros., 1958), 262.

4. Karl-Erik Warneryd and Kjell Nowak, *Mass Communication and Advertising* (Stockholm: The Economic Research Institute, 1967), 13.

5. Eugene L. Hartley and Ruth E. Hartley, "The Importance and Nature of Communications," in Charles S. Steinberg, ed., *Mass Media and Communication* (New York: Hastings House, 1966), 23.

6. Everett E. Hagen, *On the Theory of Social Change: How Economic Growth Begins* (Homewood, Ill.: The Dorsey Publishing Co., 1962), 111.

7. Ernest Dichter, *The Strategy of Desire* (Garden City, N. Y.: Doubleday & Co., 1960), 84.

8. George Horsley Smith, *Motivation Research in Advertising and Marketing* (New York: McGraw-Hill, 1954), 10.

9. A. H. Maslow, *Motivation and Personality* (New York: Harper & Row, 1954), 84.

10. Ibid., 101.

11. Walter Taplin, *Advertising: A New Approach* (Boston: Little Brown & Co., 1960), 25.

12. David C. McClelland, *The Achieving Society* (Princeton, N. J.: D. Van Nostrand Co., 1961), 99.

13. Raymond A. Bauer and Stephen A. Greyser, *Advertising in America: The Consumer View* (Boston: Division of Research, Graduate School of Business Administration, Harvard University, 1968), 67.

14. Ibid., 356.

15. Ibid., 174.

16. Ibid., 176.

17. Ibid., 181.

18. Ibid., 357.

19. Taplin, *Advertising*, 24.

20. John Kenneth Galbraith, *The Affluent Society* (Boston: Houghton-Mifflin Co., 1969), 149.

21. George Katona, *The Mass Consumption Society* (New York: McGraw-Hill, 1964), 61.

22. Raymond A. Bauer, "The Obstinate Audience: The Influence Process from the Point of View of Social Communications," in Wilbur Schramm and Donald F. Roberts, eds., *The Process and Effects of Mass Communication* (Urbana: University of Illinois Press, 1971), 326.

23. Ibid., 327.

24. The Committee on Advertising, *Principles of Advertising* (New York: Pitman Publishing Corp., 1963), 347.

25. Edgar Crane, *Marketing Communications: A Behavioral Approach to Men, Messages, and Media* (New York: John Wiley & Sons, 1965), 421.

26. Darell Blaine Lucas and Steuart Henderson Britt, *Measuring Advertising Effectiveness* (New York: McGraw-Hill, 1963), 180.

27. C. H. Sandage and Vernon Fryburger, *Advertising Theory and Practice* (Homewood, Ill.: Richard D. Irwin, 1967), 615.

28. Bogart, *Advertising*, 293.

29. Neil H. Bordon, *Advertising in Our Economy* (Chicago: Richard D. Irwin, 1945), 123.

30. Mayer, *Madison Avenue*, 312.

31. Starch, *Measuring Advertising*, 10.

32. Lucas and Britt, *Advertising Effectiveness*, 74.

33. Sandage and Fryburger, *Advertising Theory and Practice*, 577.

34. Lucas and Britt, *Advertising Effectiveness*, 176.

35. Sandage and Fryburger, *Advertising Theory and Practice*, 173.

36. Vance Packard, *The Hidden Persuaders* (New York: David McKay Company, 1957), 37.

37. Steuart Henderson Britt, *The Spenders* (New York: McGraw-Hill, 1960), 212.

38. Smith, *Motivation Research*, 75.

39. Packard, *Hidden Persuaders*, 37.

40. Bogart, *Advertising*, 58.

41. John David Lewis, "Feedback in Mass Communication: Its Nature and Use in Decision-Making," (Ph.D diss., Michigan State University), 1966.

42. Sandage and Fryburger, *Advertising Theory and Practice*, 551.

43. Marshall McLuhan, *Understanding Media: The Extensions of Man* (New York: The New American Library, 1964), 201.

44. Taplin, *Advertising*, 96.

45. Kenneth A. Longman, *Advertising* (New York: Harcourt, Brace & Jovanovich, 1971), 18.

46. Mayer, *Madison Avenue*, 11.

47. McLuhan, *Understanding Media*, 203.

48. Sandage and Fryburger, *Advertising Theory and Practice*, 5.

49. Neil H. Borden and Martin V. Marshall, *Advertising Management: Text and Cases* (Homewood, Ill.: Richard D. Irwin, 1959), 7.

50. Pierre Martineau, *Motivation in Advertising* (New York: McGraw-Hill, 1957), 13.

51. Ibid., 198.

52. McLuhan, *Understanding Media*, 205.

53. Abraham Moles, "The Future Oriented Society, Axioms and Methodology," *Futures* (December 1970), 2:4, 325.

54. Ibid.

55. John McHale, *The Future of the Future* (New York: Ballantine Books, 1971), 17.

56. John McHale, "Problems in Social and Cultural Forecasting," in Japan Society of Futurology, comp., *Challenges From the Future*, 3 vols. (Tokyo: Kodansha, 1970), I, 15.

57. Ray Brosseau, comp., *Looking Forward, Life in the Twentieth Century as Predicted in the Pages of American Magazines From 1895 to 1905* (New York: American Heritage Press, 1970).

58. Taplin, *Advertising*, 7.

59.Marshall McLuhan, *The Mechanical Bride: Folklore of Industrial Man* (New York: The Vanguard Press, 1951), 97.

60. Sanford M. Dornbusch and Lauren C. Hickman, "Other-Directedness in Consumer-Goods Advertising: A Test of Riesman's Historical Theory," *Social Forces* (October 1959), 38:1, 99.

61. Patricia Roe Morton, "Riesman's Theory of Social Character Applied to Consumer-Goods Advertising," *Journalism Quarterly* (Summer, 1967), 44:2, 337-40.

62. Ole R. Holsti, *Content Analysis for the Social Sciences and Humanities* (Reading, Mass.: Addison-Wesley Publishing Co., 1969), 60.

63. Charles E. Osgood, "The Representational Model and Relevant Research Methods," in Ithiel de Sola Pool, ed., *Trends in Content Analysis* (Urbana: University of Illinois Press, 1959), 36.

CHAPTER 6

Three motivational profiles and one forecast

THE SAMPLE OF MASS ADVERTISING

Life magazine was chosen as the carrier of the advertisements whose motivational appeals would be coded. A leader among postwar magazines, *Life* strove by means of entertaining and informative content to attract the largest possible audience for the advertising which fueled it. It was so successful at this, and so enjoyed by millions, that its demise in 1972 had the proportions of a national tragedy. As the writer of its *New York Times* obituary said:

> For slightly more than a generation, Life magazine occupied a special place in American life. . . . It was an institution that celebrated and reflected life through the second third of the 20th century and into the age of space—a big and glossy weekly that brought to millions of households and barbershops and dentists' offices (its peak circulation was more than 8.5 million) everything from moon shots to submicroscopic particles of the human anatomy.[1]

No other magazine was suitable for this study; only *Life* met the criteria of being an avowedly mass magazine which was in existence and carrying advertising during the years 1950, 1960, and 1970. That the data for all three years would be necessary is an important point worth dwelling on. Since it is social change which is to be foretold, it is motivational change which must be measured. Such change cannot be determined by comparing the frequencies of the various kinds of motivational appeals for one year alone—that is, by the relative amounts within one motivational profile. It must be done instead by looking at changes in successive profiles. By way of example, it is not enough to observe that for a given year the motive most often invoked is the need for achievement; the important factor is whether there is more or less need for achievement relative to an earlier level. From this sort of comparison would come forecasts of socio-cultural changes a decade hence. Thus, the 1960 profile, which will be the basis of the test forecast, takes on meaning only when contrasted with the 1950 data. The 1970 frequencies are needed for the construction of a forecast of the future, to 1980.

Because of these considerations the other candidates—*The Saturday Evening Post, Look, Readers' Digest*, and *TV Guide*[2]—had to be omitted. The *Post* died in 1969; its reincarnations have not been regular enough for it to be useful here. Although *Look* managed to survive until 1971, it had radically cut back its readership in the spring of 1970 to reach an exclusively high-income metropolitan audience, and so had lost its claim to being a mass magazine.[3] *TV Guide* did not appear before 1953, and the *Readers' Digest* did not permit advertising in its pages until April 1955.

All the issues of *Life* for the three target years were subjected to coding to allow for seasonal variations in the advertising. Within each issue, five full-page associative advertisements (in which whatever was being sold had been associated with something extrinsic to it) were chosen with the aid of a table of random numbers. A tabled number short of the final page number of the issue was used to select a page; the page was consulted to see if it contained an advertisement which met the criteria; the process continued until five full-page associative advertisements had been found. There were as many as fifty such advertisements per issue, so the five represented at minimum a 10 percent sample. With 260 advertisements for each year, the projected total sample contained 780, although in actuality 10 less because of double issues.

CODING PROCEDURES

A content analysis is only as good as the list of categories into which the recording units will be coded by the judges.[4] Categories must not overlap and must be able to encompass the material under study. If the categories are not mutually exclusive, data will be adulterated; if the categories are not exhaustive, data will be lost.

Since the recording units in this study are motivational appeals, the categories would have to describe the array of human needs. This is an exceedingly difficult roster to arrive at, however. It is unreasonable to hope that what are so complex and obscure as motives could be perfectly captured in tabular form. Nevertheless, the coding could not have gone on without such a list. The problem was to find, if not an ideal one, then the best that existed. By reputation this was Henry A. Murray's, constructed in the 1930s but still acclaimed: E. J. Murray, writing in 1964, stated that it remained the most influential of such lists;[5] in the 1970 edition of their *Theories of Personality*, Calvin S. Hall and Gardner Lindzey said it was "probably more widely useful than any other comparable classification."[6] Its success came about, they felt, because Murray had worked for an inclusive list which would be of maximum empirical utility.[7]

The list was the product of a well-mounted research effort, headed up by Murray, to distinguish the motives which underlie human behavior.[8] Although just a few subjects were examined, each was studied intensively through diagnostic tests and repeated interviews. From the deliberations of the members of the research team over what had been observed, the list of motives emerged.

While Murray is generally credited with the description of exactly twenty motives, a close reading of his book *Explorations in Personality* reveals that several others were also discerned. To develop a classification scheme expressly for the present study, twenty-six motives mentioned by Murray were gathered into a preliminary list of categories; this list was tried out on *Life* advertisements other than those in the sample. Motives which never seemed to be invoked, and motives which were invoked only in conjunction with other needs which clearly subsumed them, were dropped. The final list contained eighteen of Murray's needs (see Table 1).

Table 1

Categories for a Content Analysis of
Motivational Appeals in Mass Advertising,
Based on Henry A. Murray's Social Motives

Motive	Definition
Need for Achievement	To accomplish something difficult. To master, manipulate or organize physical objects, human beings, or ideas. To overcome obstacles and attain a high standard. To excel one's self. To rival and surpass others.
Need for Acquisition	To gain possessions and property. To grasp snatch, or steal things. To bargain or gamble. To work for money or goods. To keep what has been acquired.
Need for Affiliation	To draw near to another and enjoyably cooperate or reciprocate. To win affection. To adhere and remain loyal to a friend.
Need for Autonomy	To get free, shake off restraint, break out of confinement. To resist coercion and restriction. To avoid or quit activities prescribed by domineering authorities. To be independent and free to act according to impulse. To be unattached, irresponsible. To defy convention.
Need for Cognizance	To explore. To ask questions. To satisfy curiosity. To look, listen, inspect. To read and seek knowledge.

Table 1 (continued)

Categories for a Content Analysis of
Motivational Appeals in Mass Advertising,
Based on Henry A. Murray's Social Motives

Motive	Definition
Need for Deference	To admire and support a superior. To praise, honor, and eulogize. To yield to another. To emulate an exemplar. To conform to custom.
Need for Dominance	To control one's human environment. To influence or direct the behavior of others by suggestion, seduction, persuasion, or command. To dissuade, restrain, or prohibit.
Need for Exhibition	To make an impression. To be seen and heard. To excite, amaze, fascinate, entertain, shock, intrigue, amuse, or entice.
Need for Harmavoidance	To avoid pain, physical injury, illness, and death. To escape from a dangerous situation. To take precautionary measures.
Need for Inviolacy	To prevent depreciation of self-respect, to preserve one's good name, to be immune from criticism, to maintain psychological distance.
Need for Nurturance	To give sympathy and gratify the needs of someone who is weak, disabled, tired, inexperienced, etc. To feed, help, support, console, protect, comfort, nurse, heal.

Table 1 (continued)

Categories for a Content Analysis of
Motivational Appeals in Mass Advertising,
Based on Henry A. Murray's Social Motives

Motive	Definition
Need for Order	To put things in order. To achieve cleanliness, balance, arrangement, organization, neatness, tidiness, precision.
Need for Passivity	To relax, loaf, ruminate. To be disinclined to exert oneself physically and mentally.
Need for Play	To act for 'fun' without further purpose. To like to laugh and make jokes. To seek enjoyable relaxation from stress. To participate in games, sports, dancing, drinking, parties, cards.
Need for Recognition	To excite praise and commendation. To demand respect. To boast and exhibit one's accomplishments. To seek distinction, social prestige, honours, or high office.
Need for Sentience	To seek and enjoy sensuous or aesthetic impressions.
Need for Sex	To form and further an erotic relationship. To have sexual intercourse. To be in love. To hold hands, embrace, kiss.
Need for Succorance	To have one's needs gratified by sympathetic aid. To be nursed, supported, protected, loved, advised, guided, indulged, forgiven.

It was decided that the list of categories would be ready for use on the sample when concurrence among four coders who were working individually on the same blocks of twenty *Life* advertisements, again not part of the sample, averaged above .80. After each trial application, the categories were clarified with the addition of examples which the coders agreed upon (see Appendix A). Eventually intercoder reliability passed the criterion mark.

Once this point was reached, two of the four judges set out to code the 770 advertisements. Their instructions were, first, to mentally subtract from each advertisement all information which pertained directly to what was being sold, and then, to consider which of the eighteen motives were being appealed to by the material (largely pictorial) which remained. Although they were not limited in the number of assignments they could make per advertisement, neither coder judged any advertisement to contain more than three motivational appeals; the mode by far was one.

The coders felt that an advertisement for an airlines which depicted a male and female conversing across an aisle was aimed at the need for affiliation, and so coded it into that category. The Marlboro cowboy was allocated to the need for autonomy. An automobile stationed by a manorial doorway, with a woman in an evening gown lounging on the hood, was designed to invoke the need for recognition, the coders decided. The need for recognition, as well as the need for achievement, were the targets of a pictured tennis star on the court. A Coca-Cola beach party was thought to stir up the needs for play and for affiliation. The need for nurturance was appealed to in advertisements which featured pets. A product associated with Ripley's "Believe It or Not" was being sold through the need for cognizance. And so forth (see Appendix A).

Their agreement, at .82, was raised to .96 when they were asked to resolve the allocations they had differed on. Motivational appeals which they could not agree upon were not tallied.

FINDINGS

The frequencies with which the eighteen motives were invoked for each of the three years investigated appear in Table 2. To deter-

Table 2

The Chi-Square Statistic From Three Decennial
Motivational Profiles of the American Public,
Determined Through a Content Analysis of
Motivational Appeals in Mass Advertising

Motives	Observed 1950	Frequencies 1960	1970
Need for Achievement	41	29	34
Need for Acquisition	6	12	10
Need for Affiliation	80	93	54
Need for Autonomy	2	19	32
Need for Cognizance	30	13	34
Need for Deference	6	5	11
Need for Dominance	6	9	6
Need for Exhibition	10	6	9
Need for Harmavoidance	12	10	22
Need for Inviolacy	5	13	6
Need for Nurturance	24	44	22
Need for Order	3	7	4
Need for Passivity	1	5	2
Need for Play	32	35	15
Need for Recognition	64	33	23
Need for Sentience	3	2	12
Need for Sex	7	7	7
Need for Succorance	7	4	2
Totals	339	346	305

Grand Total = 990

Degrees of Freedom = 17 x 2 = 34
Chi-square = 123.35

mine the likelihood that the observed differences were due to sampling error, a chi-square test of independence was carried out. The obtained chi-square statistic (123.35, with 34 degrees of freedom) was significant at the .001 level, the critical value of 65.25 being surpassed.

The frequencies were converted to percentages, which appear in Table 3. Here the changes in motivational appeals may be clearly seen. The steepest fall over the three profiles was in the need for recognition (the need to achieve social prominence). In a sense this was mirrored by the sharpest rise, which occurred with the need for autonomy (the need to disassociate oneself from the impositions of social structures and cultural norms). These two trends speak of a steady pressure toward individuation over the postwar decades.

But aside from the need for autonomy and the need for recognition, no other motives displayed a conspicuous trend one way. Fifteen of the eighteen needs reversed direction, shifting from 1960 to 1970 in the opposite way they had moved from 1950 to 1960. There is apparently a rhythmic pattern to the succession of these profiles.

Table 3

Three Decennial Motivational Profiles of
The American Public, Expressed in Percentages

| Motives | Percentages Within Profiles | | |
	1950	1960	1970
Need for Achievement	12.1	8.4	11.1
Need for Acquisition	1.8	3.5	3.3
Need for Affiliation	23.6	26.9	17.7
Need for Autonomy	.6	5.5	10.5
Need for Cognizance	8.8	3.8	11.1
Need for Deference	1.8	1.4	3.6
Need for Dominance	1.8	2.6	2.0
Need for Exhibition	2.9	1.7	2.9
Need for Harmavoidance	3.5	2.9	7.2
Need for Inviolacy	1.5	3.8	2.0
Need for Nurturance	7.1	12.7	7.2
Need for Order	.9	2.0	1.3
Need for Passivity	.3	1.4	.7
Need for Play	9.4	10.1	4.9
Need for Recognition	18.9	9.5	7.5
Need for Sentience	.9	.6	3.9
Need for Sex	2.1	2.0	2.3
Need for Succorance	2.1	1.2	.7
Totals	100.1	100.0	99.9

THE FORECAST OF 1970

To repeat, a premise of this study is that the advertising industry, in its drive to sell, has developed an extraordinarily acute sense of what the unsatisfied needs of the American people are. Through a knowledge of the changing proportions of the various motivational appeals which the industry makes, a picture of the changing needs of the public can be drawn up. These changes in motives are held to anticipate socio-cultural change by some ten years. If this is the case, the differences between the 1950 motivational profile and the 1960 one should presage differences between the American of 1960 and that of 1970.

Table 4 presents the change in percentages between the profiles of 1950 and 1960. Looking at the differences which are greater than

Table 4

Change in the Motivational Profile of
the American Public, 1950 to 1960

Motives	Differences in Percentages
Need for Achievement	-3.7
Need for Acquisition	1.7
Need for Affiliation	3.3
Need for Autonomy	4.9
Need for Cognizance	-5.0
Need for Deference	-0.4
Need for Dominance	0.8
Need for Exhibition	-1.2
Need for Harmavoidance	-0.6
Need for Inviolacy	2.3
Need for Nurturance	5.6
Need for Order	1.1
Need for Passivity	1.1
Need for Play	0.7
Need for Recognition	-9.4
Need for Sentience	-0.3
Need for Sex	-0.1
Need for Succorance	-0.9

2 percent, it is seen that the needs for achievement and recognition, which Murray sometimes fused into a need for superiority,[9] as well as the need for cognizance (the need to seek knowledge) fell off. Those that rose were two affiliative needs, the needs for affiliation and for nurturance, and two needs which can be associated with individuality, the needs for autonomy and inviolacy (the need to maintain psychological distance).

On the basis of these changes the forecast of 1970 can be constructed. The decline in the socially assertive needs of achievement and recognition and the cerebrally assertive one of cognizance leads to a prediction of a markedly less assertive culture in 1970. Internally there would be less of a premium placed on attaining higher status or greater knowledge; externally there should be a retreat from imperialistic postures.

The decrease in striving fits a forecasted change toward a more amicable milieu in which needs for affiliation and nurturance get worked out. Congeniality should be more in evidence, and the harsher aspects of social relations mitigated. As fellowship becomes more common, the need for nurturance should produce more accommodation of the less fortunate.

Accommodation would be facilitated by more permeable social structures, the result of decreased cohesion as the needs for autonomy and inviolacy exert pressure for greater individuation. A somewhat more atomized culture could be expected. One index of this would be increasing absenteeism.

At its most terse, then, the forecast of 1970 is for a less assertive and more benign culture whose social structures are less cohesive and thus more open than those of 1960.

Now, of course, the question is, did the forecast come true? Answering this may prove to be more difficult than generating the forecast.

NOTES

1. Lawrence Van Gelder, "Drama in Photos Filled America's Window on World," *The New York Times* (December 9, 1972).

2. Mentioned in Philip H. Dougherty, "Dated Publishing Strategy Linked to Downfall of Life," *The New York Times* (December 9, 1972).

3. Ibid.

4. Ole R. Holsti, *Content Analysis for the Social Sciences and Humanities* (Reading, Mass.: Addison-Wesley Publishing Co., 1969), 95.

5. Edward J. Murray, *Motivation and Emotion* (Englewood Cliffs, N. J.: Prentice-Hall, 1964), 96.

6. Calvin S. Hall and Gardner Lindzey, *Theories of Personality,* 2d ed. (New York: John Wiley & Sons, 1970), 203.

7. Ibid., 174.

8. Henry A. Murray, *Explorations in Personality* (New York: John Wiley & Sons, 1938), 25-35.

9. Ibid., 80.

CHAPTER 7

A test of the forecast of 1970

ASSESSING 1970

Was America in 1970 a relatively open and benign society? Certainly not in the view of many critics. For them the country was epitomized by its president, Richard Nixon, one of the least open and benign of political personalities. They saw America as internally oppressive (witness race relations) and externally imperialistic (Vietnam, in a word). Theodore Roszak declared it was nothing less than totalitarian.[1] This opinion was widely thought to be confirmed by the events of May 1970, when American forces overran portions of Cambodia, students took issue, and slayings occurred at Kent State University in Ohio.

"The times are bad," lamented the journalist Harrison Salisbury in that month;[2] but then Salisbury went on to wonder if appearances were deceptive: "Symptoms of revolutionary change, systematic crises, decay of social tradition may be more acute in the United States than elsewhere; or this may simply be our own perception—

the way it seems to us."³ In the same manner the sociologist Amatai Etzioni said, "The term commonly applied to the condition in which the United States finds itself is 'crises'—urban crisis, transportation crisis, Asian crisis, educational crisis,"⁴ but later he entertained the idea that "the crises were mainly or solely in the eyes of the beholder."⁵

The possibility of a discrepancy between the fractious appearance of America and the actualities of the late sixties concerned the writers of the seminal document, *Toward a Social Report:*

> Why have income and disaffection increased at the same time? One reason is that the recent improvement in standards of living, along with new social legislation, have generated new expectations—expectations that have risen faster than reality could improve. The result has been disappointment and disaffection among a sizeable number of Americans.
>
> It is not misery, but advance, that fosters hope and raises expectations. It has been wisely said that the conservatism of destitute is as profound as that of the privileged. If the Negro American did not protest as much in earlier periods of history as today, it was not for lack of cause, but for lack of hope. If in earlier periods of history we had few programs to help the poor, it was not for lack of poverty, but because society did not care, and was not under pressure to help the poor. If the college student of the fifties did not protest as often as those of today, it was not for lack of evils to condemn, but probably because hope and idealism were weaker then.⁶

Beneath the surface of things they discerned a society which was beneficient and permeable, encouraging greater aspirations as lesser ones were fulfilled. Condemnations had more the character of irony than truth.

Their opinion was a minority one, but they were not alone in holding it. For the French social observer Jean-Francois Revel, the United States was the most estimable culture in the world, the bellwether of great cultural transformations to come.

The United States is the country most eligible for the role of
prototype-nation for the following reasons: it enjoys continuing economic prosperity and rate of growth, without
which no revolutionary project can succeed; it has technological
competence and a high level of basic research; culturally it is
oriented toward the future rather than toward the past, and it
is undergoing a revolution in behavioral standards, and in the
affirmation of individual freedom and equality; it rejects authoritarian control, and multiplies creative initiative in all do-
mains—especially in art, life style, and sense experience—and
allows the coexistence of a diversity of mutually complemen-
tary alternative sub-cultures.[7]

American transcendency owed much to "the rejection of a society
motivated by profit, dominated exclusively by economic considerations, ruled by the spirit of competition, and subjected to the mutual
aggressiveness of its members."[8] Revel would have judged the forecast of 1970 to be accurate, as probably would have F. M. Esfandiary,
who saw the forces of history producing more social fluidity, fel-
low-feeling, and individuality.[9]

Differences of opinion are of course best resolved by facts, but in
the present case, due to the size and complexity of the social unit
under study, what data there are cannot be relied upon. Those who
trust the available social statistics are likely to be "misled by inadequate interpretation of bad information based on obsolete concepts
and inadequate research and collected by underfed and overlobbied
statistical agencies."[10] The state of social indicators is such that they
can be used to support almost any position; Albert Biderman set up
a polarity of purposes which he called "indicting" and "vindicating":

General evaluative works on American society, a number of
writers have concluded, have by and large tended to dwell on
the statistical data with indicting rather than vindicating implications. Indeed, the socially vindicating musterings of statistics appear to be a relatively recent reaction to what have
been felt to be ideologically slanted indictments of American
society, or modern society in general.[11]

To show how shaky social statistics can be, Biderman analyzed the Federal Bureau of Investigation's Crime Index, which purports to show a steadily increasing incidence of criminal behavior in the United States. He concluded that

1. The errors and biasing factors effecting the Crime Index largely operate to show spurious increases, rather than decreases, in the rate.

2. The Crime Index does not provide a sound basis for determining whether criminal behavior is increasing, or decreasing, in the United States.

3. The Crime Index is highly sensitive to social developments that are almost universally regarded as improvements in the society. Thus, it is altogether possible that year-to-year increases in crime rates may be more indicative of social progress than of social decay.[12]

The index is deceptive because it is overly responsive to economic inflation (thefts of more than a $50 valuation are recorded)[13] and to the proportion of young adults in the population (the young commit the most crime; the postwar rise in births created a bulge in the figures which was to be transitory).[14] But most critically, as the disadvantaged are integrated into the society, standards of law enforcement previously unapplied to them would result in rising crime statistics.[15] A greater number of arrests would be measuring social progress, not regression.

Although social statistics will be looked to here for supporting evidence, the case should rest on less equivocal data.

An interesting if minor indicator of socio-cultural change at the end of the sixties was the public reaction to Charles Reich's book, *The Greening of America.* The book was scorned by critics, and yet sales were enormous. Philip Nobile noted, "The *vox populi* has voted Charles Reich in."[16] What readers took to was a description of something Reich called Consciousness III:

The foundation of Consciousness III is liberation. It comes

into being the moment the individual frees himself from auto-
matic acceptance of the imperatives of society and the false
consciousness which society imposes.[17]

Consciousness III does not believe in the antagonistic or competitive doctrine of life.[18]

What Consciousness III sees, with an astounding clarity that
no ideology could provide, is a society that is unjust to its
poor and minorities, is run for the benefit of a privileged few,
is lacking in its proclaimed democracy and liberty, is ugly and
artificial, that destroys environment and self, and is, like the
wars it spawns, "unhealthy for children and other living things."[19]

In stressing autonomy, regard, and harmony, Consciousness III
sounds very much like an extreme statement of what was forecasted
for American culture on the basis of the 1960 motivational profile.
Perhaps the notion of Consciousness III was so well received because
it articulated and endorsed socio-cultural changes actually going on.

A sturdier index comes from a more general phenomenon, from
the culture's surveillance activity. "Surveillance refers to the collection and distribution of information concerning events in the environment, both outside and within any particular society, thus corresponding approximately to what is popularly conceived as the
handling of news."[20] It is news which holds out the promise of an
objective source of data on the major patterns of social change, since
it is a function of the news to constantly monitor those changes.

This is not the only function of what is carried in newspapers,
needless to say. Wilbur Schramm distinguished between two varieties of news: that which is read for pleasure (such as stories of social
events, oddities, accidents, sports, recreation, and human interest),
and that which serves in the interest of general preparedness and information (such as news of public affairs, economic matters, social
problems, science, and education).[21] The latter type can be sub-
divided into first, the sort which is "instrumental to such everyday
institutional activities of the society as the stock market, navigating,
and air traffic,"[22] and second, other less routine surveillance infor-

mation. This last variety, the stuff that front pages consist of, is the kind which will be examined.

Such news makes the front page because editors have deemed it important. Explained the sociologist Robert Park:

> It is this notion of importance which seems, finally, to be the distinctive and determining specification in the conception of news. Events, if they are to have for the reader the character of news, must be not merely interesting but important. . . . The reason newspapermen know news when they see it is that they know, by a kind of instinct, what is important at a given time and place in their world and to their public.[23]

The events which are important are the events which prominently signal variation from what might be normally expected: "News is characteristically, if not always, limited to events that bring about sudden and decisive changes."[24] This being the case, if the socio-cultural environment were being distended in a certain direction, it would be reflected in increasing proportions of news stories pertaining to that alteration. If American culture exhibited in 1970 considerably more benignity and openness than it had previously more stories to do with the exercise of benignity could be expected.

This could not be told simply by examining news content of 1970. Those figures would have to be contrasted to ones from an earlier date for them to have any significance. The object would be to compare the percentage of stories relating to the exercise of openness and benignity in 1960 with the percentage in 1970. A sharp increase would help to substantiate the trial forecast.

Working with comparative data solves one considerable difficulty—the fact that news-gathering institutions do not by any means thoroughly survey the socio-cultural environment. The extraction of stories from the happenings of the culture is not done in anything like an even-handed manner, since news-gatherers are inclined toward certain traditional sources—governmental ones, to put a point on it. But this kind of bias can be allowed for by focusing on the differences between the percentage figures for the two dates.

To facilitate the test of the forecast, the motivational profiles were first reduced to the feminine-masculine dichotomy which to Sigmund Freud meant love versus aggression,[25] and to Carl Jung introversion and extraversion,[26] and to William James tender-mindedness and tough-mindedness.[27] Here the two categories were labeled benignity and assertiveness: in the first belong the more benevolent and reflective needs suiting a benign world view, and an open society; and in the second the more assertive needs that befit an understanding of the world as a place of contention, and a tightly cohering society. A panel of three psychologists was asked to divide up the list of needs; the result may be seen in Table 5.

Table 5

Henry A. Murray's Social Motives
Categorized as Benign or Assertive

Benign Needs	Assertive Needs
Need for Affiliation	Need for Achievement
Need for Autonomy	Need for Acquisition
Need for Inviolacy	Need for Cognizance
Need for Nurturance	Need for Deference
Need for Passivity	Need for Dominance
Need for Play	Need for Exhibition
Need for Sentience	Need for Harmavoidance
Need for Succorance	Need for Order
	Need for Recognition
	Need for Sex

Placing deference in the list of assertive needs was the least commonsensical of the assignments, but the panel felt that this need would indicate a restrictive culture in contrast to the open one which would emerge from the benign needs. By summing the percentages determined previously for the various needs, overall figures for benignity and assertiveness were computed. These appear in Table 6. From 1950 to 1960, needs linked with benignity and openness increased 16.7 percent. If the forecast of 1970 was accurate, there

Table 6

Percentages of Benign and Assertive Needs in Three
Decennial Motivational Profiles of
the American Public

Category of Needs	Percentages		
	1950	1960	1970
Benign	45.5	62.2	47.6
Assertive	54.6	37.8	52.3
Totals	100.1	100.0	99.9

should have been a similar rise from 1960 to 1970 in the percentage
of news stories to do with the exercise of benignity.

A CONTENT ANALYSIS OF THE NEWS

By reputation it is the *New York Times* which, of all newspapers,
takes its responsibility for surveillance most seriously. One of its
severest critics has felt called upon to admit, "A careful reader will
be able to gain a great deal of information from the *Times* that he
probably would not find in other newspapers, simply because few
of them even make a pretense of giving 'all the news that's fit to
print'."[28] In addition, the *Times,* according to Ben Bagdikian, is the
closest to a national newspaper that Americans have.[29] Its thorough-
ness and scope, therefore, made it the most suitable choice for this
study.

To get the news at its starkest, only the front page of the *Times*
was coded. It has been demonstrated that with newspapers there
is little gain to be had beyond a sample of twelve issues from any
one year,[30] so twelve front pages were selected. To allow for seasonal variations, one date per month for the years 1960 and 1970
was chosen by means of a table of random numbers. Each article
on each front page was to be coded into one of three categories
depending on whether the article pertained to matters of benignity

and openness, to assertiveness and cohesion, or to forces beyond the
volitional realm, as natural disasters.

The categories were exemplified by lists of various types of content. Informed by the efforts of Chilton Bush[31] and Edward R. Cony[32]
to enumerate varieties of newspaper content, and also by a preliminary examination of front pages which were not part of the sample,
a collection of content types was assembled. These were sorted
into the three categories by a panel of three social scientists. The
resulting coding sheet was applied by two judges to front pages
which were not to be in the sample, and the lists were further refined.

An item on the benign list, for instance, was "peace efforts," so
1970 stories on an Arab-Israeli truce would be coded here, leaving
stories on Arab-Israeli conflict to be placed in the assertive category.
The lists directed the coders to label peaceful protests—such as one
by Japanese students noted on January 16, 1960—as instances com-
patible with benignity, while protests and strikes which were not
peaceful—the storming of parliament by Japanese students on June
16, 1960—were held to suit more assertive interests. Since "sports"
was an item on the assertive list, the record-setting balloonist of
August 17, 1960, would be categorized there, while the December
10, 1970 article on the Metropolitan Opera was to be coded into the
benign group under "art and culture." (See Appendix B for the full lists.)

The two judges coded the twenty-four front pages, which were
found to contain a total of 290 stories. They agreed on the assign-
ment of all stories except 11, with the result that reliability exceeded
.96. Discussion between the judges led to the categorizing of the 11
disputed stories. An example of an ambiguous story is one on the
reorganization of the post office, which appeared in the May 23,
1970 issue; the judges ultimately placed it in the benign category.

On the basis of the observed frequencies a chi-square test of independence was carried out, as reported in Table 7. The resulting
chi-square statistic (14.57, with 2 degrees of freedom) was significant at the .001 level.

The frequencies were then converted to percentages which appear
in Table 8. The forecast of greater benignity and openness in American culture in 1970 had been based on a 16.7 percent rise from 1950 to
1960 in needs to do with benignity and individuation; since the content analysis of news reveals a comparable 17.6 percent rise from

1960 to 1970 in the exercise of benignity, the forecast is held to have been confirmed.[33] More benignity had been predicted; by this measure, more benignity occurred.

Table 7

The Chi-Square Statistic From a Content Analysis of
American News Stories in 1960 and 1970

	Observed Frequencies	
Category of Needs	1960	1970
Benign	26	45
Assertive	125	86
Other	7	1
Totals	158	132

Grand Total = 290

Degrees of Freedom = 2 x 1 = 2
Chi-square = 14.57

Table 8

Category Percentages from a Content Analysis of
American News Stories in 1960 and 1970

	Percentages	
Category of Needs	1960	1970
Benign	16.5	34.1
Assertive	79.1	65.2
Other	4.4	.8
Totals	100.0	100.1

SOME SOCIAL STATISTICS

The content analysis of the news verified the forecast for 1970 only in the most general terms, but with this demonstration as background, specific social indicators can now be consulted for whatever they can contribute. The forecast was based, it should be recalled, on falling needs for achievement, recognition, and cognizance, and rising needs for affiliation and nurturance, as well as autonomy and inviolacy.

Achievement, recognition, and cognizance all point to forms of striving—personal, social, and purely intellectual. That striving did fall off toward 1970, following the less assertive needs of 1960, is borne out by several indicators. A decreased need for cognizance depressed the growth rate of investment in new knowledge; monies for scientific research and development grew 8.3 percent annually from 1960 to 1965, then on the average of 5.2 percent annually from 1965 to 1970, and only 2.1 percent from 1970 to 1971.[34] The growth rate for patent applications slowed down in a similar fashion over the course of the decade.[35] The retarding of the society's commitment to science and technology was clearly apparent in the sharp cut-backs in funding for the space program (whose rocket launchings had been, among other things, an expressive symbol of America's prowess).[36]

Need for recognition is the need to gain high social status and the trappings that go with it; if the smaller sales of such status indicators as mink coats and luxury automobiles are any indication, this sort of struggling was far less in evidence in 1970 than in 1960. Although the annual production of automobiles increased from 6,700,000 in 1960 to 7,500,000 in 1970, Cadillac's production dropped from 159,000 to 153,000, and Chrysler Imperial's from 17,000 to 10,000.[37] Four-door sedans made up 41 percent of sales in 1960, but only 22 percent in 1970; the more modest two-door hardtops went from 11 percent of the market to 43 percent during this period.[38]

McClelland, in his book *The Achieving Society*, linked the need for achievement to economic data; they too confirm a slowdown in the culture's assertiveness at the end of the sixties. Taken in constant 1958 dollars, the Gross National Product had an average annual growth rate of 4.8 percent in the first half of the decade, 3.1 percent

in the second, and 2.7 percent for the year 1970-71.[39] Although the
rate of growth in demand for electrical power accelerated from 1960
to 1970, the rate of growth in production slowed down.[40] The decreased emphasis on assertiveness had its influence on military
spending too, even though tarter public reaction made it seem as if
the military loomed larger at the end of the decade. In actuality,
the armed services consumed 49.8 percent of the federal budget in
1960, but 40.8 percent in 1970.[41] A curtailed militarism would be
best reflected in fewer battle deaths; these did come down from a
high of 14,000 in 1968 to 4,000 in 1970.[42]

The culture grew less contentious and, conversely, more benevolent as needs for affiliation and nurturance sought satisfaction. One
index of the influence of these needs was the rise in private philanthropy, which more than doubled from $8,900 million in 1960 to
$19,400 million in 1970.[43] The growth of benignity was also sig-
naled by the treatment of convicted murderers; although the number of prisoners under sentence of death went from 210 in 1960 to
608 in 1970, the number of executions dropped from 56 to zero.[44]
Another indicator would be changes in the different kinds of volun-
tary associations, with exclusive organizations decreasing over the
decade and community- and service-oriented ones increasing. Unfortunately, appropriate figures were not collected before 1968. From
1968 to 1970, however, movement was in the direction postulated,
as fraternal organizations dropped from 640 to 610, and so-called
Greek-letter ones from 351 to 334, while educational and cultural
organizations went from 1,286 to 1,386, social welfare ones from
389 to 475, and health groups from 791 to 830.[45]

If the socio-cultural environment in 1970 was relatively more benign, a greater allocation of the nation's resources to such public
services as health, education, and welfare would be expected. This
was exactly what transpired: health expenditures went from 5.2
percent of the Gross National Product in 1960 to 7.1 percent in 1970;[46]
school expenditures had an almost identical rise, from 5.1 percent
of the GNP to 7.1 percent;[47] social welfare expenditures by the government moved from 10.6 percent of the GNP to 15.2 percent.[48]
Low rent public housing units were increasing at the rate of 4.4
percent annually at the start of the decade, and 9.4 percent at the end.[49]

Increased needs for autonomy and inviolacy in 1960 led to the prediction of more individuation in American life in 1970, and this too can be supported by social statistics. Institutions did lose their hold over their members somewhat. The percentage of the population which was married fell slightly—from 76.0 percent to 75.0 percent for males, and from 71.3 percent to 68.5 percent for females—as the percentage of single and divorced persons rose.[50] Decreasing allegiance to marriage was paralled by decreasing allegiance to employment, as revealed by absentee figures. On a typical workday in 1960, 3,200,000 workers were absent; by 1970 the number had increased by nearly 50 percent to 4,600,000.[51]

Individuation is also signaled by an increase in such self-indulgences as travel. The number of passports issued in 1960 was 853,000 and in 1970 2,219,000—growth by a factor of almost 3.[52] Visits to national parks more than doubled, up from 79 million in 1960 to 172 million in 1970.[53] Consumer expenditures for recreation also more than doubled, from $18,295 million to $39,049 million.[54] People wanted to make the most of their personal time.

And they had more of it. The average work week dropped from 38.6 hours in 1960 to 37.1 in 1970,[55] while the number of paid holidays increased from 6.9 to 7.8 for plant workers, and from 7.8 to 8.4 for office workers.[56] The culture's tendency toward greater consideration of individual workers occurred at some cost to productivity: the growth rate for output per man-hour slowed from 5.0 percent annually at the beginning of the sixties to 3.1 percent at the end, and yet the growth rate in compensation per man-hour increased from 4.3 percent annually at the beginning to 7.0 percent at the end.[57] The percentage of the total employed who engaged in work stoppages of one sort or another could also be a sign of a shift in emphasis, however slight, from the demands of the corporation to the demands of the individual: it doubled, up to 4.7 percent in 1970 from 2.4 percent in 1960.[58]

A culture which is more cordial and less contentious, a society which is more individuated and thus less rigid—these attributes speak of an open social environment in which the aspirations of the traditionally oppressed would be tolerated, even encouraged. The existence of a more benign and permeable society in 1970 than in 1960 would be testified to if gains had been realized by such groups as women and blacks.

Social indicators reveal that gains were indeed made. Women more and more resisted their conventionally ascribed subservience and established themselves in roles other than that of homemakers. They were increasingly reluctant to have more than one child: "The general picture of fertility by live birth order is one of marked decline in all but the rate for first births."[59] They were more likely to be better educated[60] and financially independent.[61] Especially telling is the fact that, while the rate of participation of males in the labor force fell off, the rate of participation of females steadily gained, and reached 42.7 percent of all women over sixteen years of age by the close of the decade.[62] (These advances have taken their toll, however, as shown by those causes of death among females which have been proportionally increasing: arteriosclerotic heart disease, cancer of the respiratory system, cirrhosis of the liver, motor vehicle accidents, suicide, and homocide.[63])

The evidence regarding the progress of blacks has been hotly debated, but according to Ben Wattenberg's careful analysis of the 1970 census data, it is unequivocal. Wattenberg stated that even though a greater number of poor blacks had become welfare recipients, this should not be interpreted as backsliding, for the percentage of blacks who could be considered poor dropped sharply from 48 percent in 1959 to 29 percent in 1970.[64] The income of black families went up nearly 100 percent in the sixties, in contrast to a 69 percent rise among white families.[65] For young married non-Southern blacks the gains were particularly striking: "The median income of black husband-wife families, in the North and West, with the head of family under 35 years of age, rose from 78 per cent of white income in 1959 to 96 per cent in 1970. There is a word to describe that figure: parity."[66] Wattenberg concluded that overall the population of blacks had become, if only by the narrowest of margins, middle class.[67]

CONCLUSION

Is it possible that variations in a people's needs are not predictive, but simply an accompaniment of socio-cultural change? That the motivational states of the public matched rather than preceded

American culture through the sixties? A more immediate relationship between needs and actualities would seem to be a reasonable conjecture: American culture in 1970, it might be argued, would suit no other needs than those in existence at the same time. But this cannot be substantiated at all with the present data, for as manifested benignity rose 17.6 percent from 1960 to 1970, benign needs fell 14.6 percent (see Table 6). Needs anticipate cultural change.

In this case, they anticipated one of the most remarkable episodes in American social history. The year 1970 is representative of a unique period, beginning in the mid-sixties and continuing to the early seventies, in which the culture saw many of its most fundamental premises undergo severe alteration with such rapidity that sparks were set off along the edges of change. Change of this magnitude cannot occur without crises, the sociologist Robert Nisbet has noted;[68] when seen as the inevitable markers of largely endorsable transformations, the crises of the late sixties can give rise to other feelings than dismay.

Forecasting the socio-cultural environment of 1970 from data antecedent by a decade was the test of the proposed forecasting method. To the extent that a content analysis of mass advertising can reveal the unsatisfied needs of the public, and to the extent that a content analysis of the news can uncover the major vectors of social change, the method has been shown to be viable. Its viability was additionally confirmed by selected social indicators. Now it can be employed to forecast the America of 1980.

NOTES

1. Theodore Roszak, *The Making of a Counter Culture* (Garden City, N. Y.: Doubleday & Co., 1969), 9.

2. Harrison Salisbury, *The Many Americans Shall Be One* (New York: W. W. Norton & Co., 1971), 13.

3. Ibid., 14.

4. Amitai Etzioni, "Introduction," in The New York Times, *Social Profile: USA Today* (New York: Van Nostrand Reinhold Co., 1970), ix.

5. Ibid., xii.

6. U.S. Department of Health, Education, and Welfare, *Toward a Social Report* (Washington, D.C.: U.S. Government Printing Office, 1969), xi.

7. Jean-Francois Revel, *Without Marx or Jesus*, trans. J. F. Bernard (Garden City, N. Y.: Doubleday & Co., 1971), 183.

8. Ibid., 209.

9. F. M. Esfandiary, *Optimism One: The Emerging Radicalism* (New York: W. W. Norton & Co., 1970).

10. Bertram M. Gross and Michael Springer, "Political Intelligence for America's Future," *The Annals of the American Academy of Political and Social Science* (March 1970), 338, 4.

11. Albert D. Biderman, "Social Indicators and Goals," in Raymond A. Bauer, ed., *Social Indicators* (Cambridge, Mass.: The MIT Press, 1966), 79.

12. Ibid., 115.

13. Ibid., 118.

14. Ibid., 122.

15. Ibid., 125.

16. Philip Nobile, ed., *The Con III Controversy: The Critic's Look at the Greening of America* (New York: Pocket Books, 1971), xi.

17. Charles A. Reich, *The Greening of America* (New York: Bantam Books, 1971), 241.

18. Ibid., 242.

19. Ibid., 246.

20. Charles R. Wright, "Functional Analysis and Mass Communication," in Lewis Anthony Dexter and David Manning White, eds., *People, Society, and Mass Communication* (New York: The Free Press, 1964), 97.

21. Wilbur Schramm, "The Nature of the News," *Journalism Quarterly* (September 1949), 26:3, 268.

22. Charles R. Wright, *Mass Communications, A Sociological Perspective* (New York: Random House, 1959), 18.

23. Robert Ezra Park, *Society: Collective Behavior, News and Opinion, Sociology and Modern Society* (Glencoe, Ill.: The Free Press, 1955), 110.

24. Ibid., 82.

25. Sigmund Freud, "Civilization and Its Discontents," *The Complete Psychological Works of Sigmund Freud*, trans. James Stachey, 23 vols. (London: The Hogarth Press, 1962), XXI, 122.

26. C. G. Jung, *Psychological Types*, trans. H. Godwin Baynes (London: Pantheon Books, 1923).

27. William James, *Pragmatism and Other Essays* (New York: Washington Square Press, 1963), 9.

28. Herman H. Dinsmore, *All the News That Fits* (New Rochelle, N. Y.: Arlington House, 1969), 18.

29. Ben H. Bagdikian, *The Information Machines: Their Impact on Men and the Media* (New York: Harper & Row, 1970), 70.

30. Guido H. Stempel, "Sample Size for Clarifying Subject Matter in Dailies," *Journalism Quarterly* (Summer 1952), 29:3, 334.

31. Chilton R. Bush, "A System of Categories for General News Content," *Journalism Quarterly* (Spring 1960), 37:2, 206-210.

32. Edward R. Cony, "Conflict-Cooperation Content of Five American Dailies," *Journalism Quarterly* (Winter 1953), 30:1, 15-22.

33. Given the gross nature of the scales employed, not too much should be made of the fact that the predicted rise and the actual rise were within 1 percent of each other. Within 5 percent would have been telling; within 10 percent would still have been indicative.

34. U.S. Bureau of The Census, *Statistical Abstract of the United States,* (Washington, D.C.: U.S. Department of Commerce, 1972), xxi (hereafter cited as *1972 Statistical Abstract*).

35. Ibid., 530.

36. Ibid., xxi.

37. Automobile Manufacturers Association, *Automobile Facts and Figures* (Detroit, Mich.: The Association, 1971), 10.

38. Ibid., 6.

39. *1972 Statistical Abstract*, xviii.

40. Ibid., xxi.

41. Ibid., 397.

42. Ibid., 260.

43. Ibid., 306.

44. Ibid., xvi.

45. Ibid., 42.

46. Ibid., 69.

47. Ibid., 105.

48. Ibid., 278.

49. Ibid., xxiii.

50. Ibid., xiii.

51. U.S. Department of Labor, *Handbook of Labor Statistics 1972* (Washington, D.C.: U.S. Government Printing Office, 1972), 72 (hereafter cited as *1972 Labor Statistics*).

52. *1972 Statistical Abstract*, 210.

53. Ibid., 201.

54. Ibid., 206.

55. *1972 Labor Statistics*, 156.

56. Ibid., 266.

57. *1972 Statistical Abstract*, xvi.

58. *1972 Labor Statistics*, 335.

59. Abbott C. Ferriss, *Indicators of Trends in the Status of American Women* (New York: Russell Sage Foundation, 1971), 65.

60. Ibid., 310.

61. Ibid., 167.

62. Ibid., 85.

63. Ibid., 240.

64. Ben J. Wattenberg and Richard M. Scammon, "Black Progress and Liberal Rhetoric," *Commentary* (April 1973), 55:4, 39.

65. Ibid., 36.

66. Ibid.

67. Ibid., 35.

68. Robert A. Nisbet, *Social Change and History: Aspects of the Western Theory of Development* (New York: Oxford University Press, 1969), 271.

CHAPTER 8

The future

THE FUTURE OF AMERICAN CULTURE

What will American culture be like at the end of the 1970s? Employing the proposed forecasting method, changes in the motivational profile of the American public through the sixties must first be established. Table 9 presents the differences in percentage between the needs of 1960 and those of 1970. Disregarding the needs that varied less than 2 percent, it is seen that affiliation, nurturance, play, and (barely) recognition decreased, while six needs increased—achievement, autonomy, cognizance, deference, harmavoidance, and sentience.

With this information the forecast of 1980 can be constructed. The first thing to be said is that there will be little tightening up of the social structures. Although the need for deference did increase slightly, pointing to somewhat less willfulness in evidence, the cohesion which social striving can contribute to a society will continue to decrease, as the need for recognition further dropped. Most influential in this connection is the strong pressure for individuation, which will result from unremitting growth in the need for autonomy. An even more atomized society can be expected and will be documented in the figures for marriage and absenteeism. Americans will increasingly be isolated from each other.

Although the cultural norms will not be those which endorse social striving, personal and intellectual achievement will be pursued,

Table 9

Change in the Motivational Profiles of
the American Public, 1960 to 1970

Motives	Differences in Percentages
Need for Achievement	2.7
Need for Acquisition	-0.2
Need for Affiliation	-9.2
Need for Autonomy	5.0
Need for Cognizance	7.3
Need for Deference	2.2
Need for Dominance	-0.6
Need for Exhibition	1.2
Need for Harmavoidance	4.3
Need for Inviolacy	-1.8
Need for Nurturance	-5.5
Need for Order	-0.7
Need for Passivity	-0.7
Need for Play	-5.2
Need for Recognition	-2.0
Need for Sentience	3.3
Need for Sex	0.3
Need for Succorance	-0.5

following the resurgence in 1970 of the needs for achievement and cognizance. The people of 1980 will go about their lives with less ostentation but more resolution. In their private ways they will be trying to improve on what they have already gained, to know more and apply it better. A renewed emphasis on science and technology should go along with a steepening of the economic growth rate.

In the more cerebral culture of 1980, the pleasures to be had will be considerably tamer than those of 1970. Because the need for play abated and the need for sentience rose, the Americans of the near future will kick up their heels less and search out contemplative aesthetic experiences more. The traditional pastimes of museums and symphonies and opera will come into their own again, while frenetic recreation and the equipment it entails will be cut back. The music of the period is not going to be as energetic or disquieting as recent music.

A less exuberant time is fast upon Americans. The reserve which will permeate the future is clearly indicated by the sharp drop in the needs for affiliation and nurturance—needs which signal the degree of interpersonal warmth and caring. The milieu of 1980 will be decidedly cooler than that of 1970. People will stay in their shells much more than is presently the case, in part because their environment will be perceived as threatening. A rise in the need for harm-avoidance from 1960 to 1970 presages a state of increased fearfulness in 1980 and will result in more money being spent on varieties of protection, as health care and military budgets.

In sum, the socio-cultural environment of 1980 will be a relatively caution-ridden one, with far less of the openness which characterized America in 1970. It will be scientifically rather than humanely oriented; social progress is going to take second billing to gains in knowledge and its applications. It will be composed of individuals coolly going about their own business, preoccupied with the private goals they have set themselves. This anomic culture will constitute a sober episode in American history.

The mention of "anomic" conjures the ghost of Emile Durkheim; perhaps it would be useful to compare the forecast of 1980 with Durkheim's concept of "anomie." Durkheim sought to describe conditions in which social solidarity had crumbled, social bonds had dissolved, and individuals were sentenced to live isolated and alienated lives.[1] So far this does resemble, if overstate, the texture of American life in 1980. However, Durkheim's "anomie" was primarily concerned with moral order and norms, or the lack of them. "Anomie" was not only an atomistic state, it was also an unregulated one, in which psychic forces usually well controlled would be heedlessly vented.[2] On this count the society of the future will not be "anomic," for those Americans will be comparatively dispassionate. Disciplined activity will be more visible, not less. Dissolution will not bring dissoluteness.

Any number of matters follow from the general forecast, but two of special interest are the lot of the oppressed within American culture and the relations of America with other countries. The society of 1980 will be even more loosely bonded, even more permeable, than that of 1970, so the aspirations of such groups as women and blacks will meet with even less resistance. The difference is going to occur in the fact that no helping hand will be extended. No longer can the oppressed count on whatever positive support they may have found in 1970; their advance will have to be exclusively due to their own efforts.

Internationally, Americans will be more likely to see other nations as threats and will therefore commit more funds to defense spending. However, diminished social cohesion will work to discourage military excursions, and the chances of war being waged will remain small. Relations with other countries will be brusque but not bellicose.

The gross scale of assertiveness and benignity which was devised to initially gauge the worth of the 1970 forecast can also be used to test the 1980 one. From 1960 to 1970 benign needs fell 14.6 percent (see Table 6); a content analysis of the news in 1980, following the procedures and categories of the content analysis executed here on the front pages of the 1970 issues of the *New York Times*, should reveal a comparable drop.

THE FUTURE OF FUTURES RESEARCH

This being the forecasted socio-cultural environment, what then of the fate of futures research within it? It will be recalled from the first chapter that Robert Theobald divided futurists into two groups—the subjectivists, who see the future as malleable, and the objectivists, for whom the future is determined by the past.[3] For the most part the subjectivists are people who wish to remake the volitional sector along more humane and democratic lines, while the objectivists are often interested in understanding the nonvolitional sector so as to anticipate change for the large-scale organizations which they frequently serve. One of these groups will lose momentum, the other will gain it, and the constitution of futures research will change.

The subjectivists have been devoted to ensuring the advent of an increasingly benign culture in which egalitarianism will reign and good will prevail. Many forms of assertiveness toward one's fellow man and one's natural environment are labeled unbecoming and are to be eliminated. At times these attitudes have ridden on an evangelical fervor which represented the extreme of the particular cultural transformations of the late sixties and early seventies. As the seventies progress, however, this interest in the caretaking of the future will be curtailed, in large part the aftermath of the descent in the need for nurturance. The numbers of people intending to seed the future with utopian communities, or to mollify existing social arrangements, will recede.

The objectivists, on the other hand, have a more dispassionate interest in the future, which is more in keeping with the temper of the times to come; their ranks are bound to swell. The rise in the need for cognizance will precede an expansion in the sort of exploration of the future which they undertake. With the need for achievement on the upswing again, the growth rate of large-scale organizations will pick up moderately, which means that skills at rational forecasting and planning will be in greater demand. In the immediate future the objectivists will displace the subjectivists.

That the study of the future will shift in the forecasted direction can be appraised by changes in the size of the audience for the publications futurists read. Those for subjectivists, such as Theobald's *Futures Conditional* or Julius Stulman's *Fields Within Fields,* should lose readers, while the more empirically inclined journals, such as *Futures* and *Technological Forecasting and Social Change,* should pick up subscribers at an increasing pace.

THE FUTURE OF THE PROPOSED
FORECASTING METHOD

Within the increasingly objective field of futures research, what is to be the role of the forecasting method devised in this study?

The chances of it achieving some popularity with forecasters appear good. It provides a relatively economical and expedient way to look ahead a decade or so for the grander patterns of socio-cultural change. Having the information derived from the proposed method as a backdrop, forecasters can then go on to examine the specific issues of interest to them and their organizations, using the methods they are accustomed to.

Methodologists and others concerned with scientific rigor will no doubt be slower to welcome it, for in their eyes the method may not have the finesse they would like to see. Although they may find it basically sound, they are likely to address themselves to aspects of it in need of more work. First, they will want to improve on the source of the data for the motivational profiles by substituting television commercials for magazine advertisements. The mode of television better suits the times, and mass magazines have apparently had their hey-day.

Second, the length of the forecasting term should be the subject of some of their questions. Although ten years seemed to work out in this study, why did it? Would a longer or shorter span be even better? Exactly what is the lag time between a need peaking and its manifestation in the culture peaking? Is the lag time the same for each of the eighteen needs?

This leads to the third area of inquiry they may take up, to do with the fit of fairly specific needs and very amorphous socio-cultural reality. The method would be much improved if particular social indicators were linked to each motive with greater precision than occurred here. If the relationship of certain needs to certain sorts of actualities could be finely described, then the method would clearly be more useful.

As refinements are incorporated into the method and more trials are executed, the chance that the logical fallacy of *post hoc ergo propter hoc* is at work here will be reduced. Despite the demonstrations in both David McClelland's work and the present study, it is still conceivable that a causative relationship between variation in a people's needs and variation in socio-cultural actualities does not exist, and that the sequence which the two studies picked up will not be found the next time out. The more the underlying concept is successfully tested, the more certain it will become that the proposed forecasting method is premised on an actual feature of socio-cultural systems.

The verifying of its rationale and refining of its procedures should ensure its acceptance among the Americans of 1980. More practical minded then their predecessors, they will want to know all they can about the nonvolitional sector, so that pragmatic action with regard to their future can be undertaken. They will not want to err on the side of arrogance, and expect too much from intervention in the systems which sustain mankind, nor on the side of submission, and expect too little. Given to neither disappointment nor resignation, they will find in mass advertising the information which can facilitate realistic forecasting and planning. Marshall McLuhan—to whom belong the last words, as the first—touched on the usefulness of advertising data for futures research when he said, "By studying the dream in our folklore, we can perhaps find the clue to understanding and guiding our world in more reasonable courses."[4]

NOTES

1. Emile Durkheim. *The Division of Labor in Society*, trans. George Simpson (New York: The Free Press, 1968), 368.

2. Emile Durkheim, *Suicide: A Study in Sociology*, trans. John A. Spaulding and George Simpson (n.p.: The Free Press of Glencoe, 1951), 253.

3. Robert Theobald, "Alternative Methods of Predicting the Future," *The Futurist* (April 1969), III:2, 45.

4. Marshall McLuhan, *The Mechanical Bride: Folklore of Industrial Man* (New York: The Vanguard Press, 1951), 50.

Categories and examples for a content analysis of motivational appeals in mass advertising

1. *Need for Achievement.* To accomplish something difficult. To master, manipulate or organize physical objects, human beings, or ideas. To overcome obstacles and attain a high standard. To excel one's self. To rival and surpass others.

"Best" of something.

Endorsement of celebrity only if advertisement depicts manner in which fame was gained, as tennis star actually playing tennis, or movie star laboring on set. Lacking this, to be coded into Recognition alone.

High standards maintained through history.

Speeding vehicles, as rocket or racing car.

Striving against nature. Against a storm, for example.

Striving in career. Example of successful (but not famous) person.

Striving in education. Schoolboy with hand up, school books, etc.

Striving in sports, either against competition, as football, or against nature, as surfing. Mere exercise, as noncompetitive swimming, is to be coded in Play.

2. *Need for Acquisition.* To gain possessions and property. To grasp, snatch or steal things. To bargain or gamble. To work for money or goods. To keep what has been acquired.

Collections, as stamps.

Contests.

Hoarding money or goods.

Prizes, money, gold.

3. *Need for Affiliation.* To draw near to another and enjoyably cooperate or reciprocate. To win affection. To adhere and remain loyal to a friend.

Children being friendly with each other.

Close warm family scene. If caretaking is suggested, also code into Nurturance. If supervision is suggested, also code into Dominance.

Couple doing something together, but not absorbed in each other. Code close physical proximity into Sex.

Friendly, but not seductive, girl.

Friendly gathering of couples, extended family, neighbors. Code large party into Play.

Friends of same sex together.

Historical scene of friendliness.

Marriage; wedding.

4. *Need for Autonomy.* To get free, shake off restraint, break out of confinement. To resist coercion and restriction. To avoid or quit activities prescribed by domineering authorities. To be independent and free to act according to impulse. To be unattached, irresponsible. To defy convention.

Exotic locales.

Fantasy scene, as Marlboro country.

Nature, as fishing.

Resisting norms; indulging oneself.

(Note: what is offered here is escape. Although escape is often solo, it can also include a companion.)

5. *Need for Cognizance.* To explore. To ask questions. To satisfy curiosity. To look, listen, inspect. To read and seek knowledge.

Different ways of life.

Maps.

Oddities and curios, as in Ripley's "Believe It or Not."

People in the act of investigating.

Questions asked and answered; explanations.

Tests, with no tangible rewards.

6. *Need for Deference.* To admire and support a superior. To praise, honor, and eulogize. To yield to another. To emulate an exemplar. To conform to custom.

A good underling featured, as secretary.

Crowd-following behavior suggested.

Directives from experts and professionals, as doctors.

Traditions emphasized, apart from quality.

7. *Need for Dominance.* To control one's human environment. To influence or direct the behavior of others by suggestion, seduction, persuasion, or command. To dissuade, restrain, or prohibit.

Central figure dominating, as Green Giant, judge.

Male commanding; female seducing.

Parents controlling children.

8. *Need for Exhibition.* To make an impression. To be seen and heard. To excite, amaze, fascinate, entertain, shock, intrigue, amuse, or entice.

Appearance stressed, as slimness, etc.

Attention-getting behavior, as standing on head, being life of party.

(Note: Exhibition, which entails being looked *at*, should be contrasted to Recognition, which involves being looked *up to*.)

9. *Need for Harmavoidance.* To avoid pain, physical injury, illness, and death. To escape from a dangerous situation. To take precautionary measures.

Old people well off, enjoying retirement.

Personnel who save from danger featured, as lifeguard, nurse, fire-
man, policeman, etc.

Threatening settings, as desert, darkness, etc.

Vulnerabilities, as Achilles heel, fire trap, etc.

10. *Need for Inviolacy.* To prevent depreciation of self-respect, to preserve one's good name, to be immune from criticism, to maintain psychological distance. To avoid humiliation. To remain or become uncriticizable by self or others.

Disordered appearance; oddball.

Formal setting which demands correct behavior, as at restaurant,
check-in-desk, formal gathering, etc.

Informal setting where "face" must be saved—"hold own in argument"; "don't be a wet blanket."

11. *Need for Nurturance.* To give sympathy and gratify the needs of someone who is weak, disabled, tired, inexperienced, etc. To feed, help, support, console, protect, comfort, nurse, heal.

Children watched over by parent.

Cute children.

Figures in need of care-taking.

Pets.

12. *Need for Order.* To put things in order. To achieve cleanliness, balance, arrangement, organization, neatness, tidiness, precision.

Cleanliness stressed.

Conspicuously studied arrangement, as with furniture.

Whiteness.

13. *Need for Passivity.* To relax, loaf, ruminate. To be disinclined to exert oneself physically and mentally.

Reclining figures; feet up.

14. *Need for Play.* To act for "fun" without further purpose. To like to laugh and make jokes. To seek enjoyable relaxaiton from stress. To participate in games, sports, dancing, drinking parties, cards.

Balloons.

Exercise and sports without competitive element; dancing.

Games.

Party.

15. *Need for Recognition.* To excite praise and commendation. To demand respect. To boast and exhibit one's accomplishments. To seek distinction, social prestige, honors, or high office.

Accouterments of high social position, as elegant settings, if outside, or elegant furnishings, if inside; elegant female companion; servants; British imagery, private airplane; etc.

Adoration of central figure, as by circle of admirers, or with ticker tape parade.

Celebrity endorsing product. If activity also shown, code into Achievement too.

(Note: to be contrasted with Exhibition.)

16. *Need for Sentience.* To seek and enjoy sensuous or aesthetic impressions.

Art work: music; etc.

Artistic setting in nature.

17. *Need for Sex.* To form and further an erotic relationship. To have sexual intercourse. To be in love. To hold hands, embrace, kiss.

Couple in close contact.

Seductive female. If she is also trying to get her way by being seductive, code into Dominance too.

18. *Need for Succorance.* To have one's needs gratified by sympathetic aid. To be nursed, supported, sustained, surrounded, protected, loved, advised, guided, indulged, forgiven, consoled. To remain close to a devoted protector. To always have a supporter.

Hearth, stove.

Person being nursed featured.

Categories and examples for a content analysis of news stories reporting the exercise of benignity or assertiveness

1. *Stories reflecting a benign and open society.*
   Art and culture
   Civil rights
   Consumer affairs
   Education
   Foreign aid
   Human interest
   International cooperation
   International neutrality
   Health
   Housing
   Environmental matters
   Minorities
   Peace efforts
   Peaceful protests and strikes
   Pensions
   Philanthropy
   Quality of life
   Removed prohibitions

Safety
Spiritual matters, other than organized religion
Wage increases
Welfare
2. *Stories reflecting an assertive and cohesive society.*
Corruption
Crime
Criminal justice systems
Enemies
Energy
Exploits
Established religion
Heads of state and their families
International conflict
National defense
Politics
Production
Protests and strikes other than peaceful
Questions of loyalty
Rebellions
Science
Space
Sports
Taxes
Technology
Transportation
3. *Other Events*
Accidents and disasters
Economic matters other than taxes and production
Weather

Bibliography

Abt, Clark C. "An Approach to Methods of Combined Sociotechnological Forecasting." *Technological Forecasting and Social Change* 2:1, 17-22.
_____. "Forecasting Future Social Needs." *The Futurist* V:1, 20-21.

Albrecht, Milton C. "Does Literature Reflect Common Values? *American Sociological Review* 21:6, 722-729.

Amara, Roy C., and Salancik, Gerald R. "Forecasting: From Conjectural Art Toward Science." *The Futurist* VI:3, 112-116.

Ament, Robert H. "Comparison of Delphi Forecasting Studies in 1964 and 1967." *Futures* 2:1, 15-23.

Appelbaum, Richard P. *Theories of Social Change.* Chicago: Markham Publishing Co., 1970.

Armbruster, Frank G. *The Forgotten Americans, A Survey of Values, Beliefs, and Concerns of the Majority.* New Rochelle, N.Y.: Arlington House, 1972.

Ayres, Robert U. *Technological Forecasting and Long Range Planning.* New York: McGraw-Hill, 1969.

Bagdikian, Ben H. *The Information Machines: Their Impact on Men and the Media.* New York: Harper & Row, 1970.

Baier, Kurt, and Rescher, Nicholas, eds. *Values and The Future*. New York: The Free Press, 1969.

Baldridge, J. Victor. "Images of the Future and Organizational Change: The Case of New York University." In Wendell Bell and James A. Mau, eds. *The Sociology of the Future*. New York: Russell Sage Foundation, 1971, 271-93.

Bauer, Raymond A. "Communication as Transaction." In Donald E. Payne, ed. *The Obstinate Audience*. Ann Arbor, Mich.: Foundation for Research on Human Behavior, 1965, 3-12.

_____. "The Communicator and the Audience." In Lewis Anthony Dexter and David Manning White, eds. *People, Society, and Mass Communications*. New York: The Free Press, 1964, 126-40.

_____. "Detection and Anticipation of Impact: The Nature of the Task." In Raymond A. Bauer, ed. *Social Indicators*. Cambridge, Mass.: The MIT Press, 1966, 1-67.

_____. "The Obstinate Audience: The Influence Process from the Point of View of Social Communications." In Wilbur Schramm and Donald F. Brooks, eds. *The Process and Effects of Mass Communications*. 2d Ed. Urbana: University of Illinois Press, 1971, 326-46.

_____, ed. *Social Indicators*. Cambridge, Mass.: The MIT Press, 1966.

_____, and Bauer, Alice H. "America, Mass Society and Mass Media." *Journal of Social Issues* XVI:3, 3-66.

_____, and Greyser, Stephen A. *Advertising in America: The Consumer View*. Boston: Division of Research Graduate School of Business Administration, Harvard University, 1968.

Beckerman, Wilfred. "The Myth of Environmental Catastrophe." *National Review*. November 24, 1972, 1293-5, 1315.

Beckwith, Burnham Putnam. *The Next 500 Years: Scientific Predictions of Major Social Trends*. New York: Exposition Press, 1967.

Beichman, Arnold. *Nine Lies About America*. London: Alcove Press, 1972.

Bell, Daniel. *The Coming of Post-Industrial Society*. New York: Basic Books, 1973.

_____. "The Measurement of Knowledge and Technology." In Eleanor Bernert Sheldon and Wilbert E. Moore, eds. *Indicators of Social Change*. New York: Russell Sage Foundation, 1968, 145-246.

_____. "The Post-Industrial Society." In Eli Ginzberg, ed. *Technology and Social Change*. New York and London: Columbia University Press, 1964, 44-59.

_____. "A Summary by the Chairman." In Daniel Bell, ed. *Toward the Year 2000: Work in Progress*. Boston: Beacon Press, 1967, 63-9.

_____. "Twelve Modes of Prediction—A Preliminary Sorting of Approaches in the Social Sciences." *Daedalus* 93:2, 845-80.

_____, ed. *Toward the Year 2000: Work in Progress.* Boston: Beacon Press, 1967.

Bell, Wendell, and Mau, James A. "Images of the Future: Theory and Research Strategies." In Wendell Bell and James A. Mau, eds. *The Sociology of the Future.* New York: Russell Sage Foundation, 1971, 6-44.

_____, and Mau, James A., eds. *The Sociology of the Future.* New York: Russell Sage Foundation, 1971.

Bennett, James. "Simulating the Future with an Econometric Model." *The Futurist* II:2, 26-27.

Bennis, Warren G., and Slater, Philip E. *The Temporary Society.* New York: Harper & Row, 1968.

Bensman, Joseph. "The Advertising Agency Man in New York." In Jeremy Tunstall, ed. *Media Sociology.* Urbana: University of Illinois Press, 1970, 202;20.

_____, and Rosenberg, Bernard. "Mass Media and Mass Culture." In Philip Olson, ed. *America as a Mass Society.* New York: The Free Press, 1963, 166-86.

Berelson, Bernard. *Content Analysis in Communication Rsearch.* Glencoe, Ill.: The Free Press, 1952.

_____, and Steiner, Gary A. *Human Behavior, An Inventory of Scientific Findings.* New York: Harcourt, Brace & World, 1964.

Bergson, Henri. *Time and Free Will.* Translated by F. L. Pogson. New York: The Macmillan Co., 1910.

Berkman, Dave. "Advertising in *Ebony* and *Life:* Negro Aspirations vs. Reality." *Journalism Quarterly* 40:1, 53-64.

Bertaux, Pierre. "The Future of Man." In William R. Ewald, Jr., ed. *Environment and Change, The Next Fifty Years.* Bloomington: Indiana University Press, 1968, 13-20.

Bestuzhev-Lada, Igor V. "Forecasting—an approach to the problems of the future." *International Social Science Journal* XXI:4, 526-534.

_____. "A Soviet Scientist Looks at Futurology." *The UNESCO Courier.* April 1971: 23-27.

Biderman, Albert D. "Social Indicators and Goals." In Raymond A. Bauer, ed. *Social Indicators,* Cambridge, Mass.: The MIT Press, 1966, 68-153.

Blum, Eleanor. *Basic Books in the Mass Media.* Urbana: University of Illinois Press, 1972.

Blumer, Herbert. "The Crowd, the Public, and the Mass." In Wilbur Schramm, ed. *The Process and Effects of Mass Communication.* Urbana: University of Illinois Press, 1965, 363-79.

Bogart, Leo. *Strategy in Advertising.* New York: Harcourt, Brace & World, 1967.

Boguslaw, Robert. *The New Utopians: A Study of System Design and Social Change.* New York: Prentice-Hall, 1965.

Borden, Neil H. *Advertising in Our Economy.* Chicago: Richard D. Irwin, 1945.

––––––. *The Economic Effects of Advertising.* Homewood, Ill.: Richard D. Irwin, 1944.

––––––, and Marshall, Martin V. *Advertising Management: Text and Cases.* Homewood, Ill.: Richard D. Irwin, 1959.

Boulding, Elise. "Futurology and the Imagining Capacity of the West." In Magorah Maruyama, ed. *1970 American Anthropological Association, Cultural Futurology Symposium: Pre-Conference Volume.* Minneapolis: University of Minnesota, 1970, 2:1-2:33.

Boulding, Kenneth. *The Meaning of the 20th Century.* New York, Evanston, and London: Harper & Row, 1964.

––––––. *The Organizational Revolution.* New York: Harper & Bros., 1953.

Brandner, Lowell, and Sistrunk, Joan. "The Newspaper: Molder or Mirror of Community Values?" *Journalism Quarterly* 43:3, 497-505.

Breed, Warren. "Analyzing News: Some Questions for Research." *Journalism Quarterly* 33:4, 467-477.

––––––. "Mass Communication and Socio-Cultural Integration." *Social Forces* 37:2, 109-16.

Bright, James R. *A Brief Introduction to Technology Forecasting.* Austin, Texas: The Pernaquid Press, 1972.

––––––. "A Few Kind Words for Trend Extrapolation." *Futures* 5:4, 344-345.

Britt, Steuart Henderson. *The Spenders.* New York: McGraw-Hill, 1960.

Brooks, Ralph M. "Social Planning and Societal Monitoring." In Leslie D. Wilcox, Ralph M. Brooks, George M. Beal, Gerald G. Klonglan, eds. *Social Indicators and Societal Monitoring.* San Francisco: Jossey-Bass, 1972, 1-49.

Brosseau, Ray. *Looking Forward, Life in the Twentieth Century as Predicted in the Pages of American Magazines from 1895 to 1905.* New York: American Heritage Press, 1970.

Brown, Harrison. *The Challenge of Man's Future.* New York: The Viking Press, 1954.

Bryson, Lyman, ed. *The Communication of Ideas.* New York: Harper & Row, 1948.

––––––, ed. *Symbols and Values: An Initial Study.* New York: Cooper Square Publishers, 1964.

Brzezinski, Zbigniew. *Between Two Ages: America's Role in the Technetronic Era*. New York: The Viking Press, 1970.

Budd, Richard W.; Thorp, Robert K.; and Donohew, Lewis. *Content Analysis of Communication*. New York: The Macmillan Co., 1967.

Bush, Chilton R. "A System of Categories for General News Content." *Journalism Quarterly* 37:2, 206;10.

Buzzi, Giancarlo. *Advertising: Its Cultural and Political Effects*. Translated by B. David Garmize. Minneapolis: University of Minnesota Press, 1968.

Calder, Nigel. "What is Future Research?" *New Scientist* 36:570, 354-5.

_____, ed. *The World in 1984*. 2 vols. Baltimore: Penguin Books, 1964.

Campbell, Angus, and Converse, Philip G., eds. *The Human Meaning of Social Change*. New York: Russell Sage Foundation, 1972.

Cantril, Albert H., and Roll, Charles W., Jr. *Hopes and Fears of the American People*. New York: Universe Books, 1971.

Cantril, Hadley. *The Pattern of Human Concerns*. New Brunswick, N.J.: Rutgers University Press, 1965.

_____. *The "Why" of Man's Experience*. New York: The Macmillan Co., 1950.

Carney, Thomas F. *Content Analysis*. Winnipeg: University of Mannitoba Press, 1972.

Carter, David E. "The Changing Face of Life's Advertisements, 1950-66." *Journalism Quarterly* 46:1, 87-93.

Casty, Alan, ed. *Mass Media and Mass Man*. New York: Holt, Rinehart & Winston, 1968.

Chaney, David. *Processes of Mass Communication*. New York: Herder & Herder, 1972.

Churchman, C. West. *Prediction and Optimal Decision, Philosophical Issues of a Science of Values*. Englewood Cliffs, N. J.: Prentice-Hall, 1961.

_____, and Ackoff, Russell L. "The Democratization of Philosophy." *Science and Society* XIII:4, 327-337.

Clarke, Arthur C. *Profiles of the Future*. New York: Bantam Books, 1967.

Clarke, I. F. "The Pattern of Prediction." *Futures* 3:3, 302-5.

Cofer, C. N., and Apley, M. N. *Motivation: Theory and Research*. New York: John Wiley & Sons, 1964.

The Committee on Advertising. *Principles of Advertising*. New York: Pitman Publishing Corp., 1963.

Cony, Edward R. "Conflict-Cooperation Content of Five American Dailies." *Journalism Quarterly* 30:1, 15-22.

Cornish, Edward S. "President's Report." *The Futurist* VII:2, 85.

————. "The Professional Futurist." In Robert Jungk and Johan Galtung eds. *Mankind 2000.* Oslo: Universitetsforlaget, 1969, 244-50.

Crane, Edgar. *Marketing Communications: A Behavioral Approach to Men, Messages and Media.* New York: John Wiley & Sons, 1965.

Dance, Frank E. X., ed. *Human Communiation Theory.* New York: Holt, Rinehart & Winston, 1967.

Danielson, Wayne A., and Wilhoit, G. C., Jr., comps. *A Computerized Bibliography of Mass Communication Research, 1944-1964.* New York: Magazine Publishers Association, 1967.

David, Henry. "Assumptions About Man and Society and Historical Constructs in Futures Research." *Futures* 2:3, 220-30.

Davison, W. Phillips. "On the Effects of Communication." *Public Opinion Quarterly* 23:3, 343-60.

DeFleur, Melvin L. *Theories of Mass Communication.* New York: McKay, 1966.

————, and Larson, Otto N. *The Flow of Information.* New York: Harper and Row, 1958.

deGrazia, Sebastian. *Of Time Work and Leisure.* New York: Twentieth Century Fund, 1962.

deHoghton, Charles, Page, William, and Streatfeild, Guy. . . . *And Now the Future, A PEP Survey of Future Studies.* London: PEP, 1971.

de Jouvenel, Bertrand. *The Art of Conjecture.* Translated by Nikita Lary. New York: Basic Books, 1967.

————. *Futuribles, Studies in Conjecture.* Geneva: Druz, vol. I, 1963, vol. II, 1965.

————. "Notes on Social Forecasting." In Michael Young, ed. *Forecasting and the Social Sciences.* London: Social Science Research Council, 1968, 118-34.

————. "Utopia for Practical Purposes." *Daedalus* 94:2, 437-52.

deTocqueville, Alexis. *Democracy in America.* 2 vols. Edited by Phillips Bradley. New York: Vintage Books, 1945.

Dewey, Edward R., and Dakin, Edwin F. *Cycles: The Science of Prediction.* New York: Henry Holt & Company, 1947.

Dexter, Lewis Anthony, and White, David Manning, eds. *People, Society and Mass Communications.* New York: The Free Press, 1964.

Dichter, Ernest. *Handbook of Consumer Motivation.* New York: McGraw-Hill, 1964.

————. *Motivating Human Behavior.* New York: McGraw-Hill, 1971.

————. *The Strategy of Desire.* Garden City, N. Y.: Doubleday & Co., 1960.

Dickson, Paul. *Think Tanks.* New York: Ballantine Books, 1971.

Dinsmore, Herman H. *All the News That Fits.* New Rochelle, N. Y.: Arlington House, 1969.

"Discussion on Future Research." In Robert Jungk and Johan Galtung, eds. *Mankind 2000.* Oslo: Universitetsforlaget, 1969, 336-43.

Dobrianov, Velichko. "On Some Theoretical and Ideological Problems of Social Forecasting, Prognostiction, and Planning." In Japan Society of Futurology, comp. *Challenges From the Future.* 3 vols. Tokyo: Kodansha, 1970, I:250-341.

Dornbusch, Sanford M., and Hickman, Lauren C. "Other-Directedness in Consumer-Goods Advertising: A Test of Riesman's Historical Theory." *Social Forces* 38:1, 99-102.

Dougherty, Philip H. "Dated Publishing Strategy Linked to Downfall of Life." *The New York Times,* December 9, 1972.

Dressler, Fritz R. S. "Subjective Methodology in Forecasting." *Technological Forecasting and Social Change* 3:4, 427-40.

Drucker, Peter F. *The Age of Discontinuity.* New York: Harper & Row, 1969.

_____. "New Technology," *The New York Times,* April 8, 1973.

Duhl, Leonard J. "Planning and Predicting: Or What to Do When You Don't Know the Names of the Variables." In Daniel Bell, ed. *Toward the Year 2000: Work in Progress.* Boston: Beacon Press, 1967, 147-56.

Duncan, Hugh Dalziel. *Communication and Social Order.* New York: The Bedminster Press, 1962.

Duncan, Otis Dudley. "Social Forecasting: The State of the Art." *The Public Interest* 17: 88-118.

Durkheim, Emile. *The Division of Labor in Society.* Translated by George Simpson. New York: The Free Press, 1968.

_____. *Suicide, A Study in Sociology.* Translated by John A. Spaulding and George Simpson. New York: The Free Press of Glencoe, 1957.

Eisenstadt, S. N. *Modernization: Protest and Change.* Englewood Cliffs, N. J.: Prentice-Hall, 1966.

Eldredge, Wentworth. "Teaching the Sociology of the Future, 1972." In Arthur M. Harkins, ed. *1972 American Sociological Association Seminar on the Sociology of the Future.* Minneapolis: University of Minnesota, Office for Applied Social Science and the Future, 1972, E:1-E:35.

Emery, F. E. "The Next Thirty Years: Concepts, Methods, and Anticipations." *Human Relations* 20:3, 199-237.

Esfandiary, F. M. *Optimism One: The Emerging Radicalism.* New York: W. W. Norton & Co., 1970.

Etzioni, Amitai. *The Active Society.* New York: The Free Press, 1968.

_____. "Introduction." In The New York Times, *Social Profile: USA Today.* New York: Van Nostrand Reinhold Co., 1970, ix-xx.

_____, and Lehman, Edward W. "Some Dangers in 'Valid' Social Measurement." In Bertram M. Gross, ed. *Social Intelligence for America's Future.* Boston: Allyn & Bacon, 1969, 45-62.

_____ and Etzioni, Eva, eds. *Social Change.* New York: Basic Books, Inc., 1964.

Ewald, William R., Jr., ed. *Environment and Change: The Next Fifty Years.* Bloomington: Indiana University Press, 1968.

_____, ed. *Environment and Policy: The Next Fifty Years.* Bloomington: Indiana University Press, 1968.

_____, ed. *Environment for Man: The Next Fifty Years.* Bloomington: Indiana University Press, 1967.

Fabun, Don. *The Dynamics of Change.* Englewood Cliffs, N. J.: Prentice-Hall, 1968.

Feinberg, Gerald. *The Prometheus Project.* New York: Doubleday & Co., 1968.

Ferkiss, Victor C. *Technological Man: The Myth and the Reality.* New York: George Braziller, 1969.

Ferriss, Abbott L. *Indicators of Trends in the Status of American Women.* New York: Russell Sage Foundation, 1971.

_____. *Indicators of Trends in American Education.* New York: Russell Sage Foundation, 1970.

_____. *Indicators of Change in the American Family.* New York: Russell Sage Foundation, 1970.

Flechtheim, Ossip. "Is Futurology the Answer to the Challenge of the Future?," in Robert Jungk and Johan Galtung, eds. *Mankind 2000.* Oslo: Universitetsforlaget, 1969, 264-9.

_____. *History and Futurology.* Meisenheim-am-Glan, Germany: Verlag Anton Hain, 1966.

Flores, Kate. "A Step for Mankind." In Arthur Harkins, ed. *1971 American Anthropological Association Experimental Symposium on Cultural Futurology: Pre-Conference Volume.* Minneapolis: University of Minnesota, Office for Applied Social Science and the Future, 1971, F:1-F:31.

Franco, G. Robert; Young, Robert A.; Moore, James A.; Wynn, Mark E.; and Leavitt, Michael R. *A General Handbook for Long-Range Environmental Forecasting.* Washington, D.C.: Policy Sciences Department, Consolidated Analysis Centers, 1973.

Fraser, J. T., ed. *The Voices of Time,* New York: George Braziller, 1966.

Freeman, Christopher. "Mathus With a Computer." *Futures* 5:1, 5-13.

Freidson, Eliot. "Communications Research and the Concept of the Mass." *American Sociological Review* 18:3, 313-17.

Freud, Sigmund. "Civilization and Its Discontents." In *The Complete Psychological Works of Sigmund Freud.* Translated by James Strachey. 23 vols. London: The Hogarth Press, 1961, XXI: 59-148.

Fuller, R. Buckminster. *Ideas and Integrities.* New York: The MacMillan Co., 1970.

———. *No More Secondhand Gods and Other Writings.* Carbondale: Southern Illinois University Press, 1963.

———. *Operating Manual for Spaceship Earth.* Carbondale: Southern Illinois University Press, 1968.

———. *Utopia or Oblivion: The Prospects for Humanity.* Bantam Books, 1969.

"Futures-Confidence from Chaos." *Futures 1:1,* 2-3.

Gabor, Dennis. *Inventing the Future.* New York: Alfred A. Knopf, 1964.

Galbraith, John Kenneth. *The Affluent Society.* Second Edition Revised. Boston: Houghton-Mifflin Co., 1969.

Galtung, Johan. "On the Future of Human Society." *Futures* 2:2, 132-42.

———, and Ruye, Mari Nolmbe. "The Structure of Foreign News." In Jeremy Tunstall, ed. *Media Sociology.* Urbana: University of Illinois Press, 1970, 259-300.

Gans, Herbert J. "The Creator-Audience in the Mass Media: An Analysis of Movie Making." In Bernard Rosenberg and David Manning White, eds. *Mass Culture.* Glencoe, Ill.: The Free Press, 1964, 315-24.

Gerbner, George. "Communication and Social Environment." *Scientific American* 227:3, 152-60.

———; Holsti, Ole R.; Krippendorff, Klaus; Pailey, William J.; and Stone, Philip J., eds. *The Analysis of Communication Content.* New York: John Wiley & Sons, 1969.

Goldhammner, Herbert. "The Social Effects of Communication Technology." In Wilbur Schramm and Donald F. Roberts, eds. *The Process and Effects of Mass Communications.* Urbana: University of Illinois Press, 1971, 897-951.

Gordon, Theodore J. *The Current Methods of Futures Research,* Middletown, Conn.: The Institute for the Future, 1971.

———. *The Future.* New York: St. Martin's Press, 1965.

———, "The Future of Futurists." *Futures* 3:4, 322-3.

———, and Ament, Robert H. *Forecasts of Some Technological and Scientific Developments and Their Societal Consequences.* Middletown, Conn.: The Institute for the Future, 1969.

Gordon, Thomas F., and Verna, Mary Ellen. *Mass Media and Socialization:*

A Selected Bibliography. Philadelphia: Temple University, School of Communications and Theatre, 1973.

Gould, Julius, and Kalb, William K., eds. *A Dictionary of the Social Sciences*. New York: The Free Press of Glencoe, 1964.

Gross, Bertram M., ed. *Social Intelligence for America's Future*. Boston: Allyn & Bacon, 1969.

_____, and Springer, Michael. "Developing Social Intelligence." In Bertram M. Gross, ed. *Social Intelligence for America's Future*. Boston: Allyn & Bacon, 1969.

_____, and Springer, Michael. "Political Intelligence for America's Future." *The Annals of the American Academy of Political and Social Science*. March 1970: 388.

Gunn, James E., ed. *Man and the Future*. Lawrence: University Press of Kansas, 1968.

Hagen, Everett E. *On the Theory of Social Change: How Economic Growth Begins*. Homewood, Ill.: The Dorsey Press, 1962.

Hall, Calvin S., and Lindzey, Gardner. *Theories of Personality*. 2d ed. New York: John Wiley & Sons, 1970.

_____, and Van de Castle, Robert L. *The Content Analysis of Dreams*. New York: Appleton-Century-Crofts, 1966.

Halmes, Paul, ed. *The Sociology of Mass Media Communicators*. Keele, Staffordshire, England: University of Keele, 1969. The Sociological Review: Monograph, No. 13.

Hansen, Donald A., and Parsons, J. Herschel, comp. *Mass Communications: A Research Bibliography*. Santa Barbara, Calif.: The Glendessory Press, 1968.

Harkins, Arthur, ed. *1971 American Anthropological Association Experimental Symposium on Cultural Futurology: Pre-Conference Volume*. Minneapolis: University of Minnesota, Office for Applied Social Science and the Future, 1971.

_____, ed. *1972 American Sociological Association Seminar on the Sociology of the Future*. Minneapolis: University of Minnesota, Office for Applied Social Science and the Future, 1972.

Harman, Willis H. "Contemporary Social Forces and Alternative Futures." *Journal of Research and Development in Education* 2:4, 67-89.

Hartley, Eugene L., and Hartley, Ruth E. "The Importance and Nature of Communication." In Charles S. Steinberg, ed. *Mass Media and Communication*. New York: Hastings House, 1966, 8-27.

Harvard University Program on Technology and Society. *A Final Review*. Cambridge, Mass.: Harvard University, 1972.

Hayashi, Yujiro. "The Direction and Orientation of Futurology as a Science." In Robert Jungk and Johan Galtung, eds. *Mankind 2000*. Oslo: Universitetsforlaget, 1969, 270-7.

Heilbroner, Robert L. *The Future as History*. New York: Harpers & Bros., 1959.

Helmer, Olaf. *In the Future State of the Union*. Menlo Park, Calif.: Institute for the Future, 1972.

_____. *Social Technology*. Contributions by Bernice Brown and Theodore Gordon. New York: Basic Books, 1966.

_____, and de Brigard, Raul. *Some Potential Societal Developments*. Middletown, Conn.: Institute for the Future, 1970.

_____, and Rescher, Nicholas. "On the Epistemology of the Inexact Science." *Management Science* 6:1, 25-52.

Henshel, Richard L. "Sociology and Prediction." *The American Sociologist* 6:3, 213-220.

Hetman, Francois. *The Language of Forecasting*. Paris: Futuribles, 1969.

Hollander, Edwin P. *Principles and Methods of Social Psychology*. New York: Oxford University Press, 1971.

Holsti, Ole R. "Content Analysis." In Gardner Lindzey and Elliot Aronson, eds. *The Handbook of Social Psychology*. 2d ed. Reading, Mass.: Addison-Wesley Publishing Co., II, 596-692.

_____. *Content Analysis for the Social Sciences and Humanities*. Reading, Mass.: Addison-Wesley Publishing Co., 1969.

Hopkins, Frank Snowden. "The United States in the Year 2000, A Proposal for the Study of the American Future." *The American Sociologist* 2:3, 149-150.

Hoselitz, Bert F., ed. *A Reader's Guide to the Social Sciences*. New York: The Free Press, 1970.

Huber, Bettina J., comp. "Studies of the Future: A Selected and Annotated Bibliography." In Wendell Bell and James A. Mau, eds. *The Sociology of the Future*. New York: Russell Sage Foundation, 1971, 339-454.

_____, and Bell, Wendell. "Sociology and the Emergent Study of the Future." *American Sociologist* 6:4, 287-95.

Huff, Toby E. "Articulating Images: The Sociology of Illusion." *Society* 10:4, 804.

Ikle, Fred Charles. "Can Social Predictions Be Evaluated?." in Daniel Bell, ed. *Toward the Year 2000: Work in Progress*. Boston: Beacon Press, 1967, 101-26.

_____. "Social Forecasting and the Problem of Changing Values." *Futures* 3:2, 146-50.

James, William. *Pragmatism and Other Essays.* New York: Washington Square Press, 1963.

Janowitz, Morris. "The Study of Mass Communication." In David L. Sills, ed. *International Encyclopedia of the Social Sciences.* 17 vols. New York: The Macmillan Co., 1968, III: 41-53.

Jantsch, Erich. *Technological Forecasting in Perspective.* Paris: Organisation for Economic Cooperation and Development, 1967.

_____. *Technological Planning and Social Futures.* New York: John Wiley & Sons, 1972.

_____. "Toward a Methodology for Systematic Forecasting." *Technology Forecasting and Social Change* 1:4, 409-19.

Japan Society of Futurology, comp. *Challenges from the Future.* Tokyo: Kodansha, 1970.

Johns-Heine, Patricke, and Gerth, Hans N., "Values in Mass Periodical Fiction, 1921-1940." In Bernard Rosenberg and David Manning White, eds. *Mass Culture,* Glencoe, Ill.: The Free Press, 1957, 226-34.

Johnston, Denis F. "Forecasting Methods in the Social Sciences." in Japan Society of Futurology, comp. *Challenges From the Future.* 3 vols. Tokyo: Kodansha, 1970, I:135-42.

Jung, Carl G. *Psychological Types.* Translated by H. Godwin Baynes. London: Pantheon Books, 1923.

Jungk, Robert. "Human Futures." *Futures* 1:1, 34-39.

_____, and Galtung, Johan, eds. *Mankind 2000.* Oslo: Universetetsforlaget, 1969.

Kahn, Herman, and Bruce-Briggs, B. *Things to Come.* New York: The Macmillan Company, 1972.

_____, and Wiener, Anthony J. "The Next Thirty-Three Years: A Framework for Speculation." In Daniel Bell, ed. *Toward the Year 2000: Work in Progress.* Boston: Beacon Press, 1967, 73-99.

_____, and Wiener, Anthony J. *The Year 2000.* The Macmillan Co., 1967.

Katona, George. *The Mass Consumption Society.* New York: McGraw-Hill, 1964.

_____. *The Powerful Consumer.* New York: McGraw-Hill, 1960.

Katz, Elihu, and Lazarsfeld, Paul F. *Personal Influence, the Part Played by People in the Flow of Mass Communications.* New York: The Free Press, 1955.

Kaufman, Felix. "Forecasting, Analysis, and Decision-Making." In Japan Society of Futurology, comp. *Challenges from the Future.* 3 vols., Tokyo: Kodansha, 1970, I:179-215.

Keller, Suzanne. "The Utility of Sociology for Futurism." In Arthur M.

Harkins, ed. *1972 American Sociological Association Seminar on the Sociology of the Future.* Minneapolis: University of Minnesota, Office for Applied Social Science and the Future, 1972, K:1-K:11.

Klapper, Joseph T. *The Effects of Mass Communication.* New York: The Free Press, 1960.

Kleppner, Otto, and Settel, Irving, eds. *Exploring Advertising.* Englewood Cliffs, New Jersey: Prentice-Hall, 1970.

Kluckhohn, Clyde, and Murray, Henry A. *Personality in Nature, Society, and Culture.* New York: Alfred A. Knopf, 1963.

Kornhauser, William. "Mass Society." In David L. Sills, ed. *International Encyclopedia of the Social Sciences,* 17 vol., New York: The Macmillan Co., 1968, 10:58-64.

Kuhn, Alfred. *The Study of Society: A Unified Approach.* Homewood, Ill.: The Dorsey Press, 1963.

Kuhns, William. *The Post-Industrial Prophets.* New York: Weybright & Talley, 1971.

Kuman, Krishnan. "Inventing the Future in Spite of Futurology." *Futures* 4:4, 369-74.

Landergren, Ulf. "Forecasting as an Aid to Planning—A Few Concepts." In Japan Society of Futurology, comp. *Challenges From the Future.* 3 vols. Tokyo: Kodansha, 1970, I:279-80.

Landers, Richard R. *Man's Place in the Dybosphere.* Englewood Cliffs, N. J.: Prentice-Hall, 1966.

Lasswell, Harold D. "The Changing Image of Human Nature: The Socio-Cultural Aspect (Future-Oriented Man)." *American Journal of Psychoanalysis* 26:2, 157-66.

_____. "The Structure and Function of Communication in Society." In Lyman Bryson, ed. *The Communication of Ideas.* New York: Harper & Row, 1948, 37-51.

_____, and Kaplan, Abraham. *Power and Society: A Framework for Political Inquiry.* New Haven: Yale University Press, 1950.

Lazarsfeld, Paul F., and Merton, Robert K. "Mass Communication, Popular Taste, and Organized Social Action." In Bernard Rosenberg and David Manning White, eds. *Mass Culture.* Glencoe, Ill.: The Free Press, 1957, 457-73.

LeLionnais, Francois. "What Future for Futurology?" *The UNESCO Courier* April 1971:4-6.

Levak, Bedrich. "The Perspectives of the Scientific and Technical Revolution." In Robert Jungk and Johan Galtung, eds. *Mankind 2000.* Oslo: Universitetsforlaget, 1969, 334-5.

Lewis, John David. "Feedback in Mass Communication: Its Nature and Use in Decision-Making." Ph.D. diss., Michigan State University, 1969.

Lindblom, C. E. "Comments on Simon." In William R. Ewald, ed. *Environment and Policy: The Next Fifty Years*. Bloomington: Indiana University Press, 1968, 384-7.

Lindzey, Gardner, ed. *Assessment of Human Motives*. New York: Holt, Rinehart & Winston, 1958.

_____, and Aronson, Eliot, eds. *The Handbook of Social Psychology*. 2d ed. 5 vols. Reading, Mass.: Addison-Wesley Publishing Co., 1968.

Little, Dennis. "Social Indicators, Policy Analysis and Simulation." *Futures* 4:3, 220-31.

Lompe, Klaus. "Problems of Futures Research in the Social Sciences," *Futures* 1:1, 47-53.

Londsdale, Richard. "Futurism: Its Development, Content, and Methodology." In the 1985 Committee of the National Conference of Professors of Educational Administration, *Educational Futurism 1985*. Berkeley: McCutchan Publishing Corp., 1971, 7-29.

Longman, Kenneth A. *Advertising*. New York: Harcourt, Brace, Jovanovich, 1971.

Long-Range Forecasting and Planning: A Sympoisum Held at the U.S. Air Force Academy, Colorado. Washington, D.C.: Department of Defense, 1966.

Lucas, Darrell, and Britt, S. H. *Advertising Psychology and Research*. New York: McGraw-Hill, 1950.

_____. *Measuring Advertising Effectiveness*. New York: McGraw-Hill, 1963.

Lundberg, Ferdinand. *The Coming World Transformation*. Garden City, New York: Doubleday & Co., 1963.

McClelland, David C. *The Achieving Society*. Princeton, N. J.: D. Van Nostrand Co., 1961.

McHale, John. *A Continuation of the Typological Survey of Futures Research U.S.* Binghamton, N. Y.: Center for Integrative Studies, 1972.

_____. *The Future of the Future*. New York: Ballantine Books, 1971.

_____. "Future Research: Some Integrative and Communicative Aspects." In Robert Jungk and Johan Galtung, eds. *Mankind 2000*, Oslo: Universetetsforlaget, 1969, 256-63.

_____. "Problems in Social and Cultural Forecasting." In Japan Society of Futurology, comp. *Challenges from the Future*. 3 vols. Tokyo: Kodansha, 1970, I:9-16.

_____. "Science, Technology, and Change." In Bertram M. Gross, ed. *Social Intelligence For America's Future*. Boston: Allyn & Bacon, 1969, 220-45.

_____. *Typological Survey of Futures Research in the U.S.* Binghamton, N. Y.: Center for Integrative Studies, 1970.

_____. *World Facts and Trends.* New York: Collier Books, 1972.

McLuhan, Marshall. "American Advertising." *Horizon* 93:4, 132-41.

_____. *Culture Is Our Business.* New York: Ballantine Books, 1972.

_____. *The Mechanical Bride: Folklore of Industrial Man.* New York: The Vanguard Press, 1951.

_____. *Understanding Media: The Extensions of Man.* New York: The New American Library, Inc., 1964.

McQuail, Denis. *Toward a Sociology of Mass Communications.* London: Collier-Macmillan, 1969.

Madden, Ward. "Forward." In Donald N. Michael, *The Unprepared Society: Planning for a Precarious Future.* New York: Basic Books, 1968, vii-xiv.

Martineau, Pierre. *Motivation in Advertising.* New York: McGraw-Hill, 1957.

Martino, Joseph P. "Computers and Technological Forecasting." *Futurist* 6:3, 205.

_____. "The Consistency of Delphi Forecasts," *The Futurists* IV:2, 63-4.

_____. "Evaluating Forecasts." *The Futurist* III:3, 75.

_____. "The Paradox of Forecasting," *The Futurist* III:1, 20.

_____. "Technology Forecasting," *IEEE Spectrum* 9-10, 32-40.

Maruyama, Magoroh, ed. *1970 American Anthropological Association Cultural Futurology Symposium: Pre-Conference Volume.* Minneapolis: University of Minnesota, 1970.

_____. "Toward a Cultural Futurology." In *American Anthropological Association Cultural Futurology Symposium: Pre-Conference Volume,* Minneapolis: University of Minnesota, 1970, Chapter 1.

Marx, Karl. *A Contribution to the Critique of Political Economy.* Translated by N. I. Stone. Chicago: Charles H. Kerr & Co., 1904.

Masini, Eleonora. *Social Forecasting.* Rome: IRADES, Edizioni Previsionali, 1972.

Maslow, A. H. *Motivation and Personality.* New York: Harper & Row, 1954.

Mayer, Martin. *Madison Avenue U.S.A.* New York: Harper & Bros., 1958.

Meadows, Donella H., Meadows, Dennis L., Randers, Jorgen, and Behrens, William W. III. *The Limits to Growth, A Report for the Club of Rome's Project on the Predicament of Mankind.* New York: Universe Books, 1972.

Meier, Richard L. *A Communications Theory of Urban Growth.* Cambridge, Mass.: The MIT Press, 1962.

Mesthene, E. G. *Technological Change.* Cambridge, Mass.: Harvard University Press, 1970.

_____. "How Technology Will Shape the Future." In William R. Ewald,

Jr., ed. *Environment and Change: The Next Fifty Years*. Bloomington: Indiana University Press, 1968, 132-52.

Michael, Donald H. *The Unprepared Society*. New York: Basic Books, 1968.

Middleton, Russell. "Fertility Values in American Magazine Fiction, 1916-1956." *Public Opinion Quarterly* 24:1, 139-43.

Miller, David C., and Hunt, Ronald L. *A Graduate-Level Survey of Futures Studies: A Curriculum Development Project*. U.S. Department of Health, Education and Welfare, Office of Education, National Center for Educational Research and Development, 1972.

Miller, S. M., and Ruby, Pamela A. *The Future of Inequality*. New York: Basic Books, 1970.

Moles, Abraham. "The Future Oriented Society, Axioms and Methodology." *Futures* 2:4, 312-26.

Moore, Wilbert G. "Forecasting the Future: The United States in 1980." *The Educational Record* 45:4, 341-54.

———. *Man, Time, and Society*. New York: John Wiley & Sons, 1963.

———. *Order and Change: Essays in Comparative Sociology*. New York: John Wiley & Sons, 1967.

———. "Predicting Discontinuities in Social Change," *American Sociological Review* 29:3, 331-38.

———. "A Reconsideration of Theories of Social Change." *American Sociological Review* 25:6, 810-18.

———. *Social Change*. Englewood Cliffs, N. J.: Prentice-Hall, 1963.

———. "Social Change." In David L. Sills, ed. *International Encyclopedia of the Social Sciences*. 17 vols. New York: The Macmillan Co., 1968, XIV, 365-75.

———. "The Utility of Utopias." *American Sociological Review*. 31; 6, 765-72.

Morton, Patricia Roe. "Riesman's Theory of Social Character Applied to Consumer-Goods Advertising." *Journalism Quarterly* 44:2, 337-340.

Mott, Frank Luther. "Trends in Newspaper Content." In Wilbur Schramm, ed. *Mass Communications*. Urbana: University of Illinois Press, 1960, 371-79.

Mumford, Lewis. *The Transformations of Man*. New York: Harper & Bros., 1956.

Murray, Edward J. *Motivation and Emotion*. Englewood Cliffs, N. J.: Prentice-Hall, 1964.

Murray, Henry A. "Components of an Evolving Personological System." In David L. Sills, ed. *International Encyclopedia of the Social Sciences*. 17 vols., New York: The Macmillan Co., 1968, XII, 5-13.

———. "Drive, Time, Strategy, Measurement, and Our Way of Life."

In Gardner Lindzey, ed. *Assessment of Human Motives.* New York: Holt, Rinehart, & Winston, 1958, 183-96.

_____. *Explorations in Personality.* New York: John Wiley & Sons, 1938.

Myrdal, Gunnar. *Value in Social Theory.* London: Routledge & Kegan Paul, 1958.

Nafziger, Ralph O., and White, David Manning, eds. *Introduction to Mass Communication Research.* Baton Rouge: Louisiana State University Press, 1963.

"The Nature and Limitation of Forecasting." In Daniel Bell, ed. *Toward the Year 2000: Work in Progress.* Boston: Beacon Press, 1967, 327-38.

The New York Times. *Social Profile: USA Today.* New York: Van Nostrand Reinhold Co., 1970.

The 1985 Committee of the National Conference of Professors of Educational Administration. *Educational Futurism 1985.* Berkeley: McCutchum Publishing Corp., 1971.

Nisbet, Robert A. *Social Change and History: Aspects of the Western Theory of Development.* New York: Oxford University Press, 1969.

_____. "The Year 2000 and All That." *Commentary* 45:6, 60-66.

Nobile, Philip, ed. *The Con III Controversy: The Critic's Look at the Greening of America.* New York: Pocket Books, 1971.

Ogburn, William F. *On Cultural and Social Change.* Edited and with an introduction by Otis Dudley Duncan. Chicago: University of Chicago Press, 1964.

_____. *The Social Effects of Aviation.* With the assistance of Jean L. Adams and S. C. Gilfillan. Boston: Houghton Mifflin Company, 1946.

Olson, Philip, ed. *America as a Mass Society.* New York: The Free Press, 1963.

Osgood, Charles E. "The Representational Model and Relevant Research Methods." in Ithiel de Sola Pool, ed. *Trends in Content Analysis.* Urbana: University of Illinois Press, 1959.

Packard, Vance. *The Hidden Persuaders.* New York: David McKay Co., 1957.

Padbury, Peter. *The Future: A Bibliography of Issues and Forecasting Techniques.* N.P.:n.n., 1971.

Park, Robert Ezra. *Society: Collective Behavior, News and Opinion, Sociology and Modern Society.* Glencoe, Ill.: The Free Press, 1955.

Parsons, Talcott, and Shils, Edward A., eds. *Toward a General Theory of Action.* Cambridge, Mass.: Harvard University Press, 1954.

_____, Shils, Edward A., and Olds, James. "Values, Motives, and Systems of Action." In Talcott Parsons and Edward A. Shils, eds. *Toward a General Theory of Action.* Cambridge, Mass.: Harvard University Press, 1952.

Payne, Donald E., ed. *The Obstinate Audience*. Ann Arbor, Mich.: Foundation for Research on Human Behavior, 1965.

"Pessimistic View of Future Issued." *The New York Times*, September 24, 1973.

Peterson, William H. "The Future and the Futurists." *Harvard Business Review* 45:6, 168-70.

Petit, Thomas A., and Zakon, Alan. "Advertising and Social Values." In Otto Kleppner and Irving Settel, eds. *Exploring Advertising*, Englewood Cliffs, N. J.: Prentice-Hall, 1960, 10-14.

Piganiol, Pierre. "Introduction: Futurology and Prospective Study." *International Social Science Journal* XXI:4, 516-25.

Platt, John. "How Men Can Shape Their Future." *Futures* 3:1, 32-47.

————. *The Step to Man*. New York: John Wiley & Sons, 1966.

Polak, Fred L. *The Image of the Future*. New York: Oceania Publications, 1961.

————. *Prognostics*. New York: Elsevier, 1970.

————. "Toward the Goal of Goals." In Robert Jungk and Johan Galtung, eds. *Mankind 2000*, Oslo: Universitetsforlaget, 1969, 307-31.

Pool, Ithiel de Sola. "Symbols, Meaning, and Social Sciences." In Lyman Bryson, ed. *Symbols and Values: An Initial Study*. New York: Cooper Square Publishers, 1964, 349-60.

————, ed. *Trends in Content Analysis*. Urbana:University of Illinois Press, 1959.

————, and Shulman, Irwin. "Newsmen's Fantasies, Audiences, and Newswriting." *Public Opinion* 23:2, 145-58.

Popper, Karl K. *The Poverty of Historicism*. New York: Harper & Row, 1964.

President's Research Committee on Social Trends. *Recent Social Trends*. 2 vols. New York: McGraw-Hill, 1933.

Raymond, Charles K. "Advertising Research." In David L. Sills, ed. *International Encyclopedia of the Social Sciences*. 17 vols. New York: Crowell Collier & Macmillan, 1968, I: 111-16.

Reich, Charles A. *The Greening of America*. New York: Bantam Books, 1971.

Rescher, Nicholas. "The Future as an Object of Research." In Kurt Baier and Nicholas Rescher, eds. *Values and the Future*. New York: The Free Press, 1969, 102-9.

————. "On Prediction and Explanation." *British Journal for the Philosophy of Science* 8:32, 281-90.

Revel, Jean-Francois. *Without Marx or Jesus*. Translated by J. F. Bernard. Garden City, N. Y.: Doubleday & Co., 1971.

Richta, Radovan. *Civilization at the Crossroads.* New York: International
Arts and Sciences Press, 1969.

_____, and Sulc, Ota. "Forecasting and the Scientific and Technological
Revolution." *International Social Science Journal* XXI:4, 563-73.

Riley, Matilda White, and Stoll, Clarice S. "Content Analysis." In David
L. Sills, ed. *International Encyclopedia of the Social Sciences.* 17 vols.,
New York: The Macmillan Co., 1968, III: 371-7.

Rivers, William L., Peterson, Theodore, and Jensen, Jay W. *The Mass Media
and Modern Society.* 2d ed. San Francisco: Rinehart Press, 1971.

Robinson, John P., and Converse, Philip E. "Social Change Reflected in the
Use of Time." In Angus Campbell and Philip E. Converse, eds. *The
Human Meaning of Social Change.* New York: Russell Sage Foundation,
1972, 17-86.

Rosenberg, Bernard, and White, David Manning, eds. *Mass Culture, The
Popular Arts in America.* New York: The Free Press, 1957.

_____. *Mass Culture Revisited.* New York: Van Nostrand Reinhold Co.,
1971.

Roszak, Theodore. *The Making of a Counter Culture.* Garden City, N. Y.:
Doubleday & Co., 1969.

Salisbury, Harrison. *The Many Americans Shall Be One.* New York: W. W.
Norton & Co., 1971.

Sandage, C. H., and Fryburger, Vernon. *Advertising Theory and Practice.*
7th ed. Homewood, Ill.: Richard D. Irwin, 1967.

_____, and Fryburger, Vernon, eds. *The Role of Advertising: A Book of
Readings.* Homewood, Ill.: Richard D. Irwin, 1960.

Sandow, Stuart. "The Pedogogy of Planning: Defining Sufficient Futures."
Futures 3:4, 324-37.

Schon, Donald A. "Forecasting and Technological Forecasting." In Daniel
Bell, ed. *Toward the Year 2000: Work in Progress.* Boston: Beacon
Press, 1967, 127-38.

Schramm, Wilbur. "The Effects of Mass Communications." In C. H. Sandage
and Vern Fryburger, eds. *The Role of Advertising.* Homewood, Ill.:
Richard D. Irwin, 1960, 204-20.

_____. "The Nature of News." *Journalism Quarterly* 26:3, 259-69.

_____. *The Science of Human Communiction.* New York: Basic Books,
1963.

_____, and Roberts, Donald F., eds. *The Process and Effects of Mass
Communication.* 2d ed. Urbana: University of Illinois Press, 1971.

Schuessler, Karl F. "Prediction." In David L. Sills, ed. *International Encyclopedia of the Social Sciences.* 17 vols., New York: The Macmillan
Co., 1968, XII: 418-25.

Science Policy Research Unit, University of Sussex. "The Limites to Growth Controversy." *Futures* 5:1, Special Issue.

Sebald, Hans. "Studying National Character Through Comparative Content Analysis." *Social Forces* 40:4, 318-22.

Seidenberg, Roderick. *Posthistoric Man.* Chapel Hill: University of North Carolina Press, 1950.

Selznick, Philip. "Institutional Vulnerability in Mass Society." In Philip Olson, ed. *America as a Mass Society.* New York: The Free Press, 1963, 13-29.

Shane, Harold G. *The Educational Significance of the Future.* Washington, D.C.: The Supplemental Program of the World Future Society, 1972.

Sheldon, Eleanor Bernert, and Freeman, Howard E., "Notes on Social Indicators: Promises and Potential." *Policy Sciences* 1:1, 97-111.

_____, and Moore, Wilbert E. "Monitoring Social Change in American Society." *Indicators of Social Change.* New York: Russell Sage Foundation, 1968, 3-24.

_____. *Indicators of Social Change.* New York: Russell Sage Foundation, 1968.

Shils, Edward. "The Theory of Mass Society." In Philip Olson, ed. *America as a Mass Society.* New York: The Free Press, 1963, 30-47.

Shostak, A. B., and Pennington, A. S. "Methodology: Futurism Pro and Con." *Futures* 3:2, 173-6.

Simon, Herbert A. "Research for Choice." In William R. Ewald, Jr., ed. *Environment and Policy: The Next Fifty Years.* Bloomington: Indiana University Press, 1968, 360-87.

Simon, Julian L. *Basic Research Methods in Social Science.* New York: Random House, 1969.

Sisk, John P. "The Future of Prediction." *Commentary* 49:3, 65-68.

Smith, George Horsley. *Motivation Research in Advertising and Marketing.* New York: McGraw-Hill, 1954.

Smoker, Paul. "Social Research for Social Anticipation." *American Behavioral Scientist* 12:6, 7-13.

Sorokin, Pitirim A. *The Basic Trends of Our Times.* New Haven: College and University Press, 1964.

_____. *Social and Cultural Dynamics.* Revised and Abridged in One Volume by the Author. Boston: Porter Sargent, Publishers, 1957.

Starch, Daniel. *Measuring Advertising Readership and Results.* New York: McGraw-Hill, 1966.

Stempel, Guido H. "Sample Size for Clarifying Subject Matter in Dailies." *Journalism Quarterly* 29:3, 333-34.

Stephenson, William, "The 'Infantile' vs the 'Sublime' in Advertisements." *Journalism Quarterly* 40:2, 181-86.

———. *The Play Theory of Mass Communication.* Chicago: University of Chicago Press, 1967.

Stulman, Julius. *Evolving Mankind's Future.* Philadelphia: J. B. Lippincott Co., 1967.

Taplin, Walter. *Advertising: A New Approach.* Boston: Little Brown & Co., 1960.

Taylor, Charles Lewis, and Hudson, Michael C. *World Handbook of Political and Social Indicators.* 2d ed. New Haven: Yale University Press, 1972.

Teilhard de Chardin, Pierre. *The Future of Man.* Translated by Norman Denny. New York: Harper & Row, 1964.

Theobald, Robert. *An Alternative Future for America II.* Chicago: The Swallow Press, 1970.

———. "Alternative Methods of Predicting the Future." *The Futurist* III:2, 43-47.

Thompson, William Irwin. *At the Edge of History.* New York: Harper & Row, 1971.

Toffler, Alvin. "The Future as a Way of Life." *Horizon* VII:3, 109-15.

———. Future Shock. New York: Random House, 1970.

———, ed. *The Futurists.* New York: Random House, 1972.

Touraine, Alain. *The Post-Industrial Society/Tomorrow's Social History: Classes, Conflicts and Culture in the Programmed Society.* Translated by Leonard F. X. Mayhew. New York: Random House, 1971.

Tunstall, Jeremy, ed. *Media Sociology.* Urbana: University of Illinois Press, 1970.

U.S. Bureau of the Census. *Statistical Abstract of the United States.* Washington, D.C.: U.S. Department of Commerce,. 1972.

U.S. Bureau of the Census, U.S. Department of Commerce. *The Statistical History of the United States From Colonial Times to the Present.* Stamford, Conn.: Fairfield Publishers, 1965.

U.S. Department of Health, Education, and Welfare. *Toward a Social Report.* Washington, D.C.: U.S. Government Printing Office, 1969.

U.S. Department of Labor. *Handbook of Labor Statistics 1972.* Washington, D.C.: U.S. Government Printing Office, 1972.

Van Gelder, Lawrence, "Drama in Photos Filled America's Window on World." *The New York Times.* December 9, 1972, 16.

Vickers, Sir Geoffrey. *Value Systems and Social Change.* New York: Basic Books, 1968.

Wallia, C. S., ed. *Toward Century 21: Technology, Society, and Human Values.* New York: Basic Books, 1970.

Warneryd, Karl-Erik, and Nowak, Kjell. *Mass Communication and Advertising*. Stockholm: The Economic Research Institute, 1967.

Wasserman, Paul; Allen, Eleanor; and Georgi, Charlotte. *Statistical Sources*. Detroit: Gale Research Co., 1971.

Wattenberg, Ben J., and Scammon, Richard M. "Black Progress and Liberal Rhetoric." *Commentary* 55:4, 35-44.

Weaver, W. Timothy. "The Delphi Forecasting Method," *Phi Delta Kappan* LII:1, 267-71.

Webb, Eugene J.; Campbell, Donald T.; Schwartz, Richard D.; and Sechrest, Lee. *Unobtrusive Measures, Nonreactive Research in the Social Sciences*. Chicago: Rand McNally & Co., 1966.

Weber, Max. *The Protestant Ethic and the Spirit of Capitalism*. Translated by Talcott Parsons. New York: Charles Scribner's, 1930.

Weiner, Bernard. *Theories of Motivation: From Mechanism to Cognition*. Chicago: Markham, 1972.

Westley, Bruce H. "Scientific Method and Communication Research." In Ralph O. Nafziger and David M. White, eds. *Introduction to Mass Communication Research*. Baton Rouge: Louisiana State University Press, 1963, 238-76.

_____, and Maclean, Malcolm. "A Conceptual Model for Communications Research." *Journalism Quarterly* 34:1, 31-38.

"What Do Futurists Study?" *The Futurist* 1:1, 5.

Wiener, Norbert. *Cybernetics, or Control and Communication in the Animal and the Machine*. Cambridge, Mass.: The MIT Press, 1948.

_____. *The Human Use of Human Beings, Cybernetics and Society*. New York: Avon Books, 1967.

Wilcox, Leslie D.; Brooks, Ralph M.; Beal, George M.; and Klonglan, Gerald E. *Social Indicators and Societal Monitoring*. San Francisco: Jossey-Bass, 1972.

Williams, Robin M., Jr. *American Society, A Sociological Interpretation*. 2d ed. rev. New York: Alfred A. Knopf, 1967.

_____. "Individual and Group Values." In Bertram M. Gross, ed. *Social Intelligence for America's Future*. Boston: Allyn & Bacon, 1969, 163-87.

Wilson, Albert, and Wilson, Donna. "Toward the Institutionalization of Change." In Magoroh Maruyama, ed., *Cultural Futurology Symposium: Pre-Conference Volume*. Minneapolis: University of Minnesota, 1970, Chapter 12.

Winthrop, Henry. "The Sociologist and the Study of the Future." *The American Sociologist* 3:2, 136-145.

_____. "Utopia Construction and Future Forecasting: Problems, Limitations, and Relevance." In Wendell Bell, and James A. Mau, eds. *The Sociology of the Future*. New York: Russell Sage Foundation, 1971, 78-105.

_____. *Ventures in Social Interpretation*. New York: Appleton-Century-Crofts, 1968.

Wirth, Louis. "Consensus and Mass Communication," *American Sociological Review* 13:1, 1-15.

Wolfenstein, Martha, and Leites, Nathan. *Movies: A Psychological Study*. Glencoe, Ill.: The Free Press, 1950.

Wren-Lewis, John, "Faith in the Technological Future." *Futures* 2:3, 258-62.

Wright, Charles R. "Functional Analysis and Mass Communication." In Lewis Anthony Dexter and David Manning White, eds. *People, Society and Mass Communications*. New York: The Free Press, 1964, 91-109.

_____. *Mass Communiction: A Sociological Perspective*. New York: Random House, 1959.

Wright, John S., Warner, Daniel S., and Winter, Willis L., Jr. *Advertising*. New York: McGraw-Hill, 1971.

_____. *Speaking of Advertising*. New York: McGraw-Hill, 1963.

Wrong, Dennis H. "On Thinking About the Future." *The American Sociologist* 9:1, 26-31.

Wynn, Mark. "Who Are the Futurists?" *The Futurist* VI:2, 73-77.

Yaker, Henry; Osmond, Humphry; and Cheek, Frances, eds. *The Future of Time: Man's Temporal Environment*. New York: Doubleday & Co., 1971.

Young, Michael. "Forecasting and the Social Sciences." In Michael Young, ed., *Forecasting and the Social Sciences*, London: Social Science Research Council, 1968, 1-36.

_____, ed. *Forecasting and the Social Sciences*. London: Social Science Research Council, 1968.

Zeman, Milos. "Futurology—Illusion or Reality?" *Futures* 3:1, 6-10.

Index

ABOUT THE AUTHOR

Jib Fowles is chairman of the Studies of the Future Department, University of Houston at Clear Lake City. He has written a number of articles on aspects of futures research and is currently editing a *Handbook of Futures Research* to be published by Greenwood Press.